USING dBASE III Plus™

Leonard Presby

HOUGHTON MIFFLIN COMPANY BOSTON

Dallas Geneva, Illinois Palo Alto Princeton, New Jersey

ISBN: 0-395-47796-4

Printed in the U.S.A.

HIJ-SM-9543210

Contents

Preface

Using dBASE III Plus introduces the student to one of the most popular database management application programs available today. While this program provides users with powerful analytical tools, its very complexity and sophistication can make dBASE III Plus difficult to learn. The comprehensive reference manual supplied with the commercial version of the software explains all of its features but can be difficult for the beginner to fully under stand. Most existing manuals also provide too much detail and are overwhelming to the student. This manual offers the beginning user practical instruction in the fundamental operations of dBASE III Plus.

The most important feature of the book is its clear focus on its intended audience—beginning students. The manual is

- written for the beginner
- practical
- modular

For the most part, rarely used and esoteric features that are unlikely to be needed by many students are excluded, eliminating a major source of confusion found in typical all-inclusive manuals. Emphasis is on those features that are essential to understanding the use and structure of dBASE III Plus.

Clear, hands-on instructions walk students through each element of the program. After being introduced to the basic concepts and terminology necessary to run dBASE III Plus, students are shown how to use the ASSIST, which makes dBASE III Plus function like a menu-based program. In this way students avoid the anxiety of having to learn commands in order to start using the program. Beginning with the ASSIST, students gain confidence as well as an understanding of how the program is supposed to perform. Only then are they introduced to the program's command structure. New keystrokes are highlighted at the beginning of each chapter, and exercises allow students to test their understanding of the program.

The manual teaches students how to create a database structure; use dBASE III commands to look at information; add, update, and remove records; change the appearance of the database; rearrange and search for data; generate reports; and work with custom screens. A quick reference guide concludes the manual.

Because the manual teaches both the ASSIST menu and the command structure, the student is provided with a practical understanding of database management applications. At the same time, the manual's modular structure allows it to be easily tailored to a specific course. Instructors can assign the most appropriate features for their particular course, and students who are interested in exploring the program in greater detail can easily do so.

The educational version of dBASE III Plus supplied with this manual has been limited in the following ways: (1) the word DEMO appears in addition to the dot, and (2) you may only store 31 records. This number is more than sufficient for classroom instruction and practice. Except for these two limitations, the educational version of dBASE III Plus performs exactly like the commercial version.

To use this software, you must have the following:

- A copy of the master disks containing the educational version of dBASE III Plus supplied to instructors adopting this manual
- An IBM-PC or compatible computer that uses double-sided disks
- At least 256K RAM (Random Access Memory)
- MS DOS 2.11 or PC DOS 2.0, 2.1, or 3.x
- Two disk drives: drive A holds the dBASE III Plus applications disk, and drive B holds a data disk (a hard disk can also be used)
- A color or black and white monitor
- Formatted, double-sided floppy disks for backing up the program disk and storing data

Use of a printer is optional.

Loading dBASE III PLUS

The End-User Agreement allows you to copy the software into RAM, install the Software onto a permanent storage device (hard disk), or make copies to floppy for the purpose of backup. You should always make backup copies of all of your software. At some point in time the hard disk or the diskette drive that you are using will fail. They are *electro-mechanical* devices and therefore will break down sometime in the future. Backing up the programs and data is your way of avoiding disaster. If you have a backup you can always recover in the event of a failure.

The program is distributed on two floppy disks and by copying the program to hard disk you will have backed up the files. Following are instructions to load the dBASE III PLUS software onto a hard disk. (Consult your DOS manual for instructions on using COPY and FORMAT if you wish to make copies of the program to floppies.) Installing the software on a hard disk will also allow for much faster program access.

We assume that you know how to get your hard disk system up and running: how to get to the root directory C> prompt. When you have the C> prompt on the screen follow the steps below to load dBASE III PLUS onto your hard drive. WARNING . . . System Disks 1 and 2 from USING dBASE III PLUS both contain an INSTALL.BAT. If you use that batch you will replace the CONFIG.SYS file on your hard disk and you probably don't want to do that. Use the following routine to avoid inadvertently overwriting any of your hard disk files.

- Make a directory to hold the dBASE III PLUS files by typing **md\demo_db3** and pressing Return (Note: the \ character is the backslash NOT the frontslash, and the _ character is the underline NOT the dash.)

- Change to the newly created directory, that is, make it active by typing **cd\demo_db3** and pressing Return
- Insert USING dBASE III PLUS System Disk 1 into floppy drive A: and close the drive door
- Type **copy a:*.*** and press the Return key
- You should see a message saying the 10 files were copied
- Insert USING dBASE III PLUS System Disk 2 into floppy drive A: and close the drive door
- Type **copy a:*.*** and press the Return key
- You should see a message saying the 4 files were copied. You have transferred the dBASE III PLUS files to your hard drive.

To start the program make sure you are in the demo_db3 directory, type **dbase** and press the Return key.

Publisher's Foreword

This book is in the Houghton Mifflin Software Solutions Series. The series is explicitly designed to offer solutions to the problems encountered by educators who wish to include instruction on popular commercial application software programs as a component of courses they teach.

The purpose of this series is to provide high quality, inexpensive—in fact, remarkably inexpensive—tutorial manuals keyed to the leading software packages available.

Instructionally Innovative

Each manual in the Software Solutions Series focuses on those features of a particular program that will actually be used by most individuals. The manuals do not purport to teach everything there is to know about the product; to do that, the manual would have to be needlessly complex and would impose unrealistic time constraints on both students and instructors. The manuals will enable students to attain comfortable proficiency in the use of software products.

Flexible

The Software Solutions Series permits instructors to choose the manuals that best suit their needs. This offers an important advantage over those manual that combine coverage of several programs in a single publication and thus limit flexibility.

Cost

Students enrolled in a computer literacy or business data processing course often require lab-based instruction on the use of three or more application programs, usually a word processing program, a database manager, and a spreadsheet program. This common course configuration can impose a financial burden on students if they must purchase three expensive manuals in addition to the primary course text. We believe the Software Solutions Series goes a long way toward solving this problem by providing an effective and inexpensive method for learning about software.

High Quality

All manuals in the Software Solutions Series are authored by writers who have teaching experience in the classroom and in training programs in business and industry. Each manual in the series has been reviewed for accuracy and pedagogical effectiveness.

Software Disks

The Software Solutions Series currently consists of fourteen manuals and the following software products.

Master disks containing educational versions of V-P Planner Plus, Microsoft Works, WordPerfect 4.2, WordStar, dBASE III Plus, and SuperCalc 4 are available from Houghton Mifflin without charge to adopters of the manuals. These disks may be duplicated for individual student use by instructors in accordance with applicable license agreements.

For Lotus 1-2-3, WordPerfect 5.0, Microsoft Word, MS-DOS, dBASE IV, Lotus 1-2-3 Release 2.2, BASIC and PageMaker, data disks rather than educational versions of the program disks are available from Houghton Mifflin without charge to adopters.

All manuals in the Software Solutions Series are for use with IBM equipment except for PageMaker, which is only for the Macintosh.

We wish to thank Microsoft Corporation, WordPerfect Corporation, MicroPro International, Computer Associates, Ashton-Tate and Paperback Software for their cooperation in helping to make this series available.

End-user Agreement

Important: Please read this page before using the dBASE III Plus program, a copy of which is being made available to you for use in conjunction with this Textbook pursuant to the terms of this Agreement for educational, training and/or demonstration purposes.

EXCLUSIONS OF WARRANTIES AND LIMITATIONS OF LIABILITY

THE COPY OF THE dBASE III PLUS PROGRAM MADE AVAILABLE FOR USE WITH THIS TEXTBOOK IS A LIMITED FUNCTIONALITY VERSION OF dBASE III PLUS, AND IS INTENDED SOLELY FOR EDUCATIONAL, TRAINING AND DEMONSTRATION PURPOSES. ACCORDINGLY, THIS COPY OF dBASE III PLUS IS PROVIDED "AS IS," WITHOUT WARRANTY OF ANY KIND FROM ASHTON-TATE OR HOUGHTON MIFFLIN COMPANY. ASHTON-TATE AND HOUGHTON MIFFLIN COMPANY HEREBY DISCLAIM ALL WARRANTIES OF ANY KIND WITH RESPECT TO THIS LIMITED FUNCTIONALITY COPY OF dBASE III PLUS, INCLUDING WITHOUT LIMITATION THE IMPLIED WARRANTIES OF MERCHANTABILITY AND FITNESS FOR A PARTICULAR PURPOSE. NEITHER ASHTON-TATE NOR HOUGHTON MIFFLIN COMPANY SHALL BE LIABLE UNDER ANY CIRCUMSTANCES FOR CONSEQUENTIAL, INCIDENTAL, SPECIAL OR EXEMPLARY DAMAGES ARISING OUT OF THE USE OF THIS LIMITED FUNCTIONALITY COPY OF dBASE III PLUS, EVEN IF ASHTON-TATE OR HOUGHTON MIFFLIN COMPANY HAS BEEN APPRISED OF THE LIKELIHOOD OF SUCH DAMAGES OCCURRING. IN NO EVENT WILL ASHTON-TATE'S OR HOUGHTON MIFFLIN'S LIABILITY (WHETHER BASED ON AN ACTION OR CLAIM IN CONTRACT, TORT OR OTHERWISE) ARISING OUT OF THE USE OF THIS LIMITED FUNCTIONALITY COPY OF dBASE III PLUS EXCEED THE AMOUNT PAID FOR THIS TEXTBOOK.

LIMITED USE SOFTWARE LICENSE AGREEMENT

The term "Software" as used in this agreement means the Limited Use version of dBASE III Plus which is made available for use in conjunction with this Textbook solely for educational, training and/or demonstration purposes. The term "Software Copies" means the actual copies of all or any portion of the Software, including backups, updates, merged or partial copies permitted hereunder.

PERMITTED USES

You may:

- Load into RAM and use the Software on a single terminal or a single workstation of a computer (or its replacement).
- Install the Softwarc onto a permanent storage device (a hard disk drive).
- Make and maintain up to three back up copies provided they are used only for back-up purposes, and you keep possession of the back-ups. In addition, all the information appearing on the original disk labels (including copyright notice) must be copied onto the back-up labels.

This license gives you certain limited rights to use the Software and Software Copies for educational, training and/or demonstration purposes. You do not become the owner of and Ashton-Tate retains title to, all the Software and Software Copies. In addition, you agree to use reasonable efforts to protect the Software from unauthorized use, reproduction, distribution or publication.

All rights not specifically granted in this license are reserved by Ashton-Tate.

USES NOT PERMITTED

You may not:

- Make copies of the Software, except as permitted above.
- Rent, lease, sublicense, time-share, lend or transfer the Software, Software Copies or your rights under this license except that transfers may be made with Ashton-Tate's prior written authorization.
- Alter, decompile, disassemble, or reverse-engineer the Software.
- Remove or obscure the Ashton-Tate copyright and trademark notices.

DURATION

This agreement is effective from the day you first use the Software. Your license continues for fifty years or until you return to Ashton-Tate the original disks and any back-up copies, whichever comes first.

If you breach this agreement, Ashton-Tate can terminate this license upon notifying you in writing. You will be required to return all Software Copies. Ashton-Tate can also enforce our other legal rights.

GENERAL

This agreement represents the entire understanding and agreement regarding the Software and Software Copies and supersedes any prior purchase order, communication, advertising or representation.

This license may only be modified in a written amendment signed by an authorized Ashton-Tate officer. If any provision of this agreement shall be unlawful, void, or for any reason unenforceable, it shall be deemed severable from, and shall in no way affect the validity or enforceability of the remaining provisions of this agreement. This agreement will be governed by California law.

Please sign and return this agreement to: Legal Affairs Dept., Ashton-Tate Corporation, 20101 Hamilton Avenue, Torrance, CA 90502–1319.

____

(Signature)

1

Introduction: Basic Terminology

At the end of this chapter you should know

- **what a database is.**
- **why you might want a database to help make life easier.**

We, as students or businesspersons, may want to keep information on taxes, customers, purchases, inventory, personnel, and so on. A filing system typically will hold information we may need, and if we create the system well, we should be able to find, use, analyze, and make any changes. Unfortunately, file cabinets use quite a bit of space, and sometimes more than one department or individual needs the same data. For example, the dean's office in a college might want to know the names of all students on the Honors List from Fall 1987, or a financial office might want to know what and how many students are on scholarship. Information that can answer both questions is probably located in two physically distinct areas of the campus. For one individual to get answers to both questions, two trips to different departments will be necessary. Fortunately, a database manager can help solve the problem of wasted time, effort, and space. A database manager can be considered a computerized filing system. dBASE III PLUS, one such computerized filing system, allows us to deal with much larger amounts of data than we could do manually, and in a more efficent manner as well. (dBASE III PLUS is also a computer language for writing programs, but we will not discuss that here.) dBASE III PLUS can be used to simplify, analyze, find, examine, report, sort, modify, update, delete, and cross-reference, just to mention a few of its many operations.

Let us look at the following typical example. A university would like to keep information on people who are phoned for donations to the institution. One way some of the information could be organized is in list form:

Donor number: 18
Donor Name: David Dunn
Address: 17 Main St.
Boston Mass. 02176
Phone: 617–566–2345

Each data item, such as a donor name, is called a **field.** A group of related fields forms a **record.** A **file** is a group of related records.

Another way of organizing this information is in table form:

DNUM	LAST	FIRST	ADDRESS	CITYSTATE	ZIP	PHONE
18	Dunn	David	17 Main St.	Boston Mass.	02176	617–566–2345
19	Byrd	Ava	24 Ave. A.	Boston Mass.	02176	617–566–7968
20	Cho	Bob	4 Well Ave.	Boston Mass.	02176	617–566–5939

This table can be considered a database file, where each column is a field and each row represents a record.

The university might want to maintain another file, one that has details on the pledges; it could look like this:

DNUM	PAIDUP	DONORSINCE	DATECALLED	ITEMPROMIS	PURPOSE	VALUE
20	T	1978	10/3/87	Currency	Scholarship	$25
32	F	1985	11/3/87	Stock	None	$200
39	T	1986	11/14/87	Art	Gym	$600

Each donor would be assigned a donor number (DNUM).

The school would like to know if the donor's dues are paid up to date (PAIDUP). A question could be, Since when has the person been a donor (DONORSINCE)? The school would also like to know when each person was called for a pledge (DATECALLED). What type of item was promised (ITEMPROMISED)? Does this item go toward a particular purpose, or is it just a general donation (PURPOSE)? What is the value of the item promised (VALUE)?

A database consists of many interrelated fields. A **relational database,** such as dBASE III PLUS, organizes data elements into two-dimensional tables of rows and columns. In the above example, DNUM is the field that relates both files. A database manager can help us search, update, and add all the records at one time, thus eliminating the examining of each file for updating purposes. It can all be done in one step. dBASE III PLUS can draw on many different files as long as the files are linked by a common field. In our example, we can find out what Mr. Dunn pledged by searching the second file for the donor number that corresponds to his name in the first file. Note that we do not have to have his name written two times in each field; we can obtain this information once there is a link between the fields.

Other information could be obtained from these files. When you give the right commands, you can, for example:

1. Print a report of donors broken down by city.
2. Issue a summary report of how much money has been promised.
3. Send reminders to all donors who have not paid up their pledges.
4. Send special letters of thanks to those who have donated at least ten times in amounts greater than $10.
5. Print a report on items pledged, broken down by item categories.
6. Print a list of names, phone numbers, and items promised in ascending order by names.
7. Print names and phone numbers broken down by local telephone exchange numbers.
8. Sort all items donated in descending order of value.
9. Update the people who are now married.

2

Running dBASE III PLUS

At the end of this chapter you should

- **know how to get dBASE III PLUS up and running.**
- **understand the ASSIST menu with its submenus.**

Important commands or keys in this chapter:

- **ASSIST**
- **F1 key**

Running dBASE III PLUS

From floppy:

[1] Boot the system: First put the DOS diskette in drive A, close the door, and turn on the computer. Do not forget to turn the monitor on also; you can leave the printer off for the time being. Enter the date and time and wait for the A>.

[2] Place the dBASE III PLUS System Disk 1 diskette in drive A. Type DBASE and press the Enter key. Follow the instructions on the screen and press the Enter key one more time.

From hard disk:

[1] Follow the guidelines given by the instructor to boot the hard disk.

[2] Most likely you will only need to select a menu choice if running from a hard disk.

You should now see a menu similar to that shown in Figure 2.1.

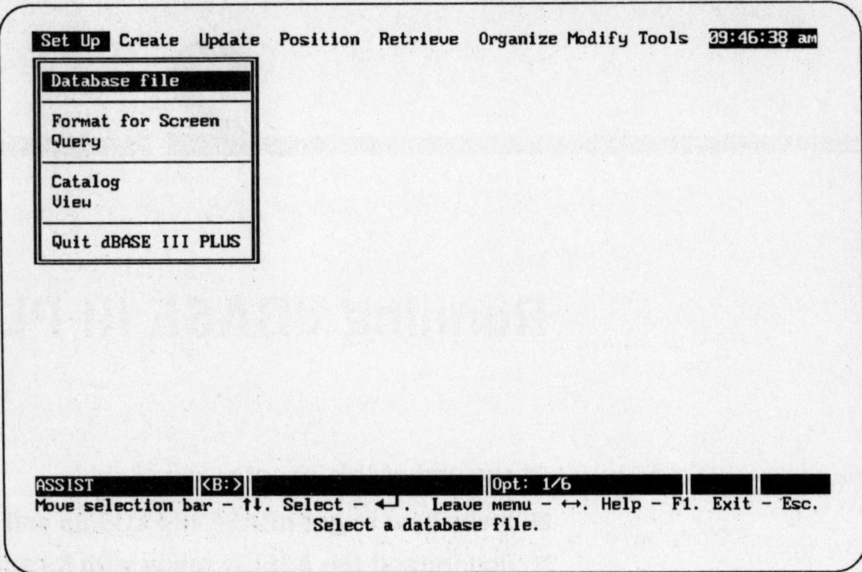

Figure 2.1 dBASE III PLUS starting menu.

Congratulations! You are now in the dBASE program. You have reached the ASSIST menu, which will make it even easier for you to learn how to learn dBASE. Typically, you use dBASE by issuing commands. The ASSIST menu, also known as a pulldown menu, simplifies this procedure by prompting you with these commands. Thus, you do not have to memorize the commands or look them up in the manual. After you become familiar with this method, you can continue to use it or go right into using commands without this menu.

You should now see a menu similar to that shown in Figure 2.1.

You see eight menu choices at the top of the screen as well as the current time. The reverse video shows that the Set Up option is being selected.

Choice 1: Set Up

Below Set Up is a submenu that lets you choose more options that all relate to Set Up. The reverse video is highlighting Database file. If you wish to choose any of the other choices in the submenu, move the up and down arrows.

Notice the bottom of the screen. There are three lines of information:

Line 1 is called the status bar. It shows that the ASSIST menu is being used and also shows the current disk drive (<B:>), the file in use (it is blank right now), the current submenu option or record number, and, finally, the status of the Ins (insert) and Caps Lock (blank right now).

Line 2 is called the navigation line. It tells you how to navigate or move about between menu or submenu options.

Line 3 is called the message line. If you do not know what to do, check this line.

Choice 2: Create

This choice lets you create new database files as well as designs for screen layouts.

Choice 3: Update

This choice lets you make changes to the records in the database.

Choice 4: Position

This choice helps you move to the part of the database you would like to view or change.

Choice 5: Retrieve

This choice shows information in the database in use. In addition, it enables you to sum, count, and find an average.

Choice 6: Organize

This choice allows you to change the order of the data you are seeing.

Choice 7: Modify

This choice allows you to change the design of the database.

Choice 8: Tools

This choice lets you see the file names and enables you to copy, rename, and erase files.

Moving Between Menus

You can move between menus either by pressing the left and right arrow keys or by typing the first letter of the name in the menu selection. For example, to use the Tools option, press T.

If You Make a Mistake

To cancel a choice, press the Esc (escape) key. The Esc key brings you back one level to the previous submenu choice. If you press Esc twice, you are out of the ASSIST mode. To get back into the ASSIST mode, type ASSIST.

If You Need Help

If you want more information about almost anything you need in dBASE, press function key 1, F1. You will see information corresponding to what you chose on the menu. To return to the menu, press the Esc key once.

On Your Own

1. Move between menus by pressing the appropriate arrows.
2. Move between items in the submenus by pressing the appropriate arrows.
3. Choose the Tools choice by choosing the appropriate letter.
4. Change the disk drive from B to drive A.

3

Using the ASSIST

At the end of this chapter you should know

- **how to create a file.**
- **how to save a file.**
- **how to move the pointer around the file.**
- **the difference between LIST and DISPLAY.**

You are now ready to set up a database file. Let us go back to the earlier example—the first donor file:

DNUM	LAST	FIRST	ADDRESS	CITYSTATE	ZIP	PHONE
18	Dunn	David	17 Main St.	Boston Mass.	02176	617–566–2345
19	Byrd	Ava	24 Ave. A.	Boston Mass.	02176	617–566–7968
20	Cho	Bob	4 Well Ave.	Boston Mass.	02176	617–566–5939

Remember that the rows are records and the columns are fields. You will soon be entering a list of ten donors.

1 Create. The first step is to highlight the Create option in the menu at the top of the screen. Notice that Database file is highlighted and in the status bar you see Opt 1/6 (see Figure 3.1).

Touch Enter. Note that Create appears on the bottom of the screen above the status line. You have just issued the command CREATE without any real

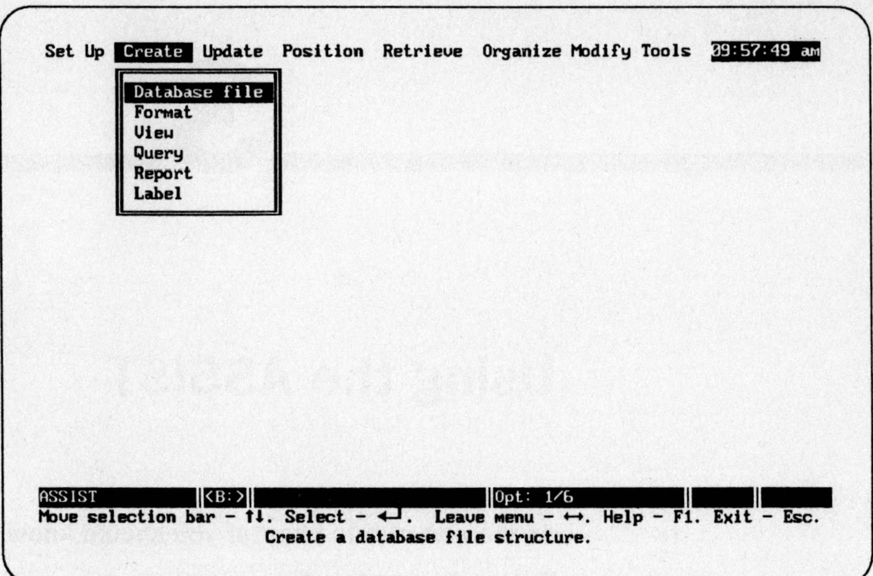

Figure 3.1 The CREATE menu.

typing. When you use the command mode (next chapter) instead of ASSIST, you will actually type this command.

2 Choose the disk drive. Probably disk drive B is currently highlighted. (If there is no blank formatted disk in the selected drive, put one in there now.) Choose the data drive by moving the up or down arrows and press Enter. This is the drive where your database will be stored.

3 Name your file. Every file you use must have a unique name. This file we are using could logically be called DONOR. Type the word in either lower- or uppercase (dBASE does not care) and press the Enter key.

NOTE: If you want to name the file something else, that is okay, but there are some rules you should be aware of. Only eight characters are allowed. The first character must be a letter; the other seven characters can be any combination of letters and digits or the underscore. Spaces, however, are not allowed.

4 Set up the structure. As you remember, dBASE sets up your data in table fashion, where the rows are records and the columns are fields. You must define this structure so that dBASE knows exactly what you are calling each field, where the data will be located, and what this data looks like. dBASE allows fields to consist of any or all of the following:

Character: this field holds any text including blanks, punctuation, and symbols, for example, LAST for last name or ADD for address.

Numeric: this field holds numbers and plus and minus signs. It will not accept commas or $.

Date: this field holds the date in the form mm/dd/yy.

Logical: this field holds true, false, yes, no (T/F/Y/N).

Memo: this field holds text for notes.

Let us apply this information to our example. All the fields in the file DONOR are character. You may ask, How about zip code or donor number; aren't these characters numeric? The rule is that any field that contains numbers but will not be used for calculations is classified as character.

Enter DNUM for the first field and press the Enter key. To change the type of field to numeric, for example, just touch the space bar. To get back to where you were, touch the space bar a few times, noting the field-type changes that are possible. Choose character by touching Enter. Touch the Enter key and choose a width size appropriate for the largest donor number you might expect. Use a width of 5, which will handle 99,999 numbers. Press the Enter key and you are ready for the next field. Enter the remaining fields:

Field Name	Type	Width
LAST	Character	15
FIRST	Character	10
ADDRESS	Character	20
CITYSTATE	Character	15
ZIP	Character	5
PHONE	Character	12

5 Save the structure. When the last width has been entered, press the Enter key three times to complete this file. You have now saved the structure of this file and are now ready to enter some data.

NOTE: If you later decide you would like to modify this structure by adding another field, it is very easy to do so. We cover this subject in Chapter 7.

You could answer "yes" to the question on the screen and start entering. Instead, say "no" by pressing N; you are now back at the ASSIST menu.

Take a five-minute break.

Welcome back. It is now time to enter data. To begin, choose Set Up, press Enter, and then choose the data drive. Select DONOR as your file and Enter. Press Enter when asked if the file is indexed. (More on this later.) Choose Update and then Append. Your screen should show a blank template. You are now ready to enter data. You will be typing the data for each field in the reverse video blank area. Watch your capitals when entering the data.

NOTE: dBASE automatically beeps when you have data that fill the whole field, such as Zip code, and dBASE flips into the next record after the phone number has been entered.

DNUM	LAST	FIRST	ADDRESS	CITYSTATE	ZIP	PHONE
39	Dunn	David	17 Main St.	Boston Mass.	02176	617–566–2345
32	Byrd	Ava	24 Ave. A.	Boston Mass.	02176	617–566–7968
20	Cho	Bob	4 Well Ave.	Boston Mass.	02176	617–566–5939
105	Ray	John	12 Grand Pl.	Boston Mass.	02176	617–566–2121
93	Gold	Mary	312 Wind St.	Cambridge Mass.	02138	617–567–1458
102	Ray	Joan	18 Ash St.	Cambridge Mass.	02171	617–566–5365
13	Lieb	Sue	8 Wesson Ave.	Quincy Mass.	02169	617–566–2174
95	Wolf	Bob	21 Boyle St.	Brookline Mass.	02176	617–566–6992
100	Jones	Frank	65 Oak St.	Newton Mass.	02163	616–566–3811
91	Rite	Gary	99 Pearl St.	Brookline Mass.	02176	617–566–7243

TIP: If you want to view an earlier record to make sure you have entered the data on that record, just press the PgUp (page up) key. Press PgDn (page down) to return to a later record.

Save the data by pressing Enter.

The POSITION Menu

When you call up a file, dBASE points to the first record. You can have that pointer move around by choosing various selections in the POSITION submenu. Let us take a look at it (see Figure 3.2).

The record where the pointer is positioned is the one that is listed in the status bar after that record. You can see the record you are on as well as how many records are in the database.

Now try some of the many possibilities for moving the pointer around:

1. If you want to go to record 1, choose Position, Goto Record, Top (*note:* the status line shows rec 1/10).
2. If you want to go to record 7, choose Goto Record, Record, 7 (*note:* the status line shows 7/10).
3. If you want to skip to record 9, choose Skip, 2.

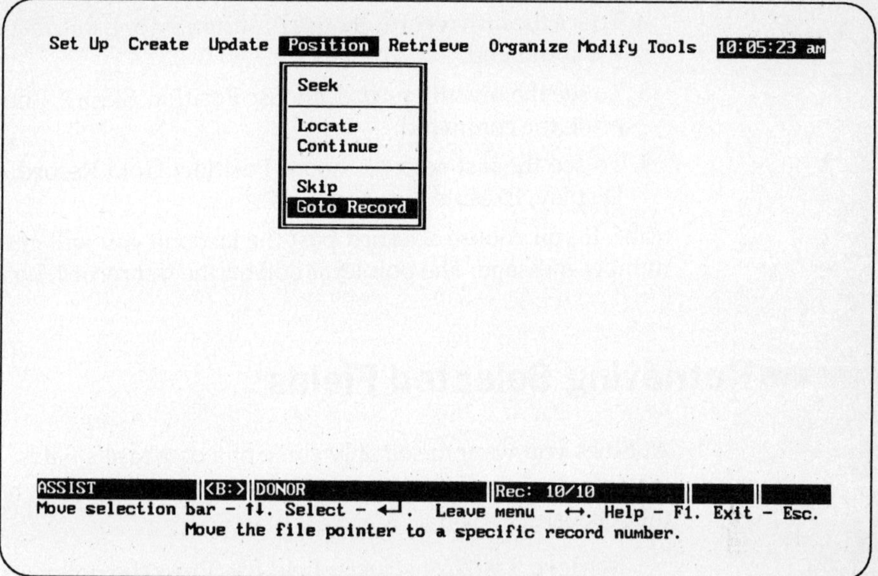

Figure 3.2 Position option with submenus.

4. If you want to go back three records, choose Skip, –3.
5. If you want to go to the last record, choose Goto Record, Bottom.

The RETRIEVE Menu

Typically we would like to look at the data rather than only point to it. Select Retrieve from the ASSIST menu and then choose List. Now choose Execute the command and press Enter. (Do not direct the output to the printer yet.) That is all there is to do.

NOTE: The difference between List and Display is that List shows all the records in the entire file from the top to the bottom, whereas Display is usually used to show only the current record. Also note that records appear on two lines; they wrap around the screen. This is because our file contains 82 characters, and that is more than can be displayed on a monitor.

Try a few examples:

1. To see the first record, choose Position, Goto Record, Top, Retrieve, Display, Execute the command.

2. To see the fifth record, choose Position, Skip, 4, Retrieve, Display, Execute the command.
3. To see the seventh record, choose Position, Skip, 2, Retrieve, Display, Execute the command.
4. To see the last record, choose Position, Goto Record, Bottom, Retrieve, Display, Execute the command.

NOTE: If you choose a record past the last one you will get an invalid record number message. The pointer is still on the last record, however.

Retrieving Selected Fields

At times you want to see only some of a database's fields. For example, you may want a list of donors with their telephone numbers, nothing else. To do this, choose:

Retrieve, List, Construct a field list. Press the down arrow once. Choose Last by pressing the Enter key; choose First by pressing the Enter key; choose Phone by pressing the down arrow three times and then pressing the Enter key. Press the right arrow. See Figure 3.3. (Note the command line shows the command entered by these keystrokes.) Choose Execute the command and press the Enter key (see Figure 3.4). Answer N to the printer message.

At times you want to see just a partial list of records.

You can do this by using Specify scope, which is used regularly with List and Display. When you use Specify scope, you can choose All, Next n [number], Record n [number], and Rest.

Let us see how it works.

NOTE: Remember that at times you might have to bring the pointer back to the beginning of the file. (This is done by choosing Position, Goto Record, Top.) If you do not return the pointer, it will be pointing to the present record.

To see just the first five records of your file, choose Retrieve, List, Specify scope, Next, 5, Execute the command, and Enter.

To see the remaining records of your file, choose List, Specify scope, Rest, Execute the command, and Enter.

To see a list of the first four records of the file, choose Retrieve, List, Specify scope, Next, 4, Construct a field list, Last, First, move arrow to the right, Execute the command, and Enter (see Figure 3.5). (If this did not work, check to see if you positioned the pointer at the top of the file before you issued the RETRIEVE command.)

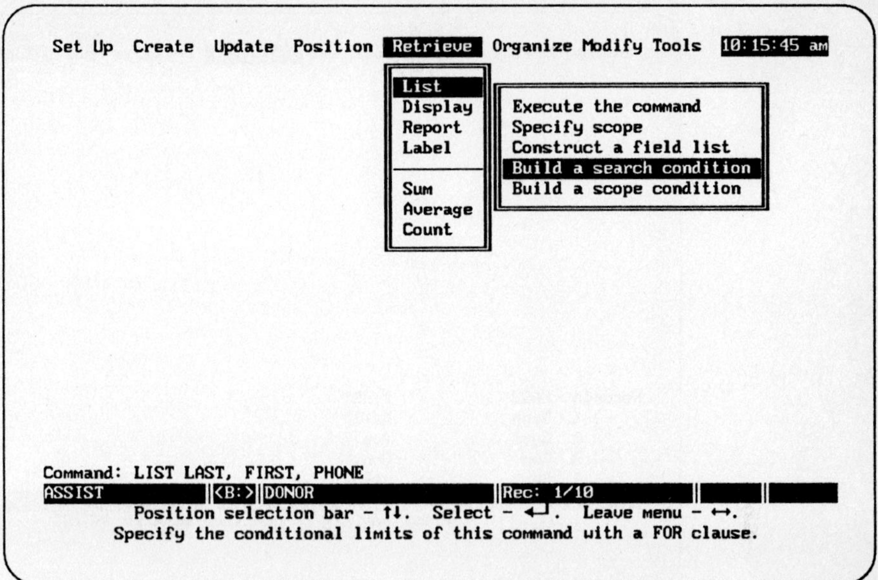

Figure 3.3 Commands used for retrieving selected fields.

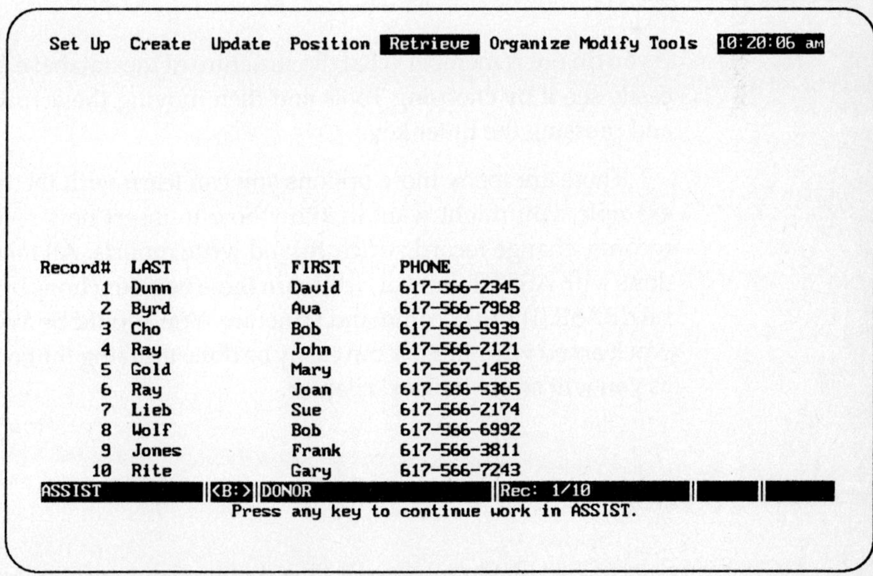

Figure 3.4 Result of retrieving selected fields.

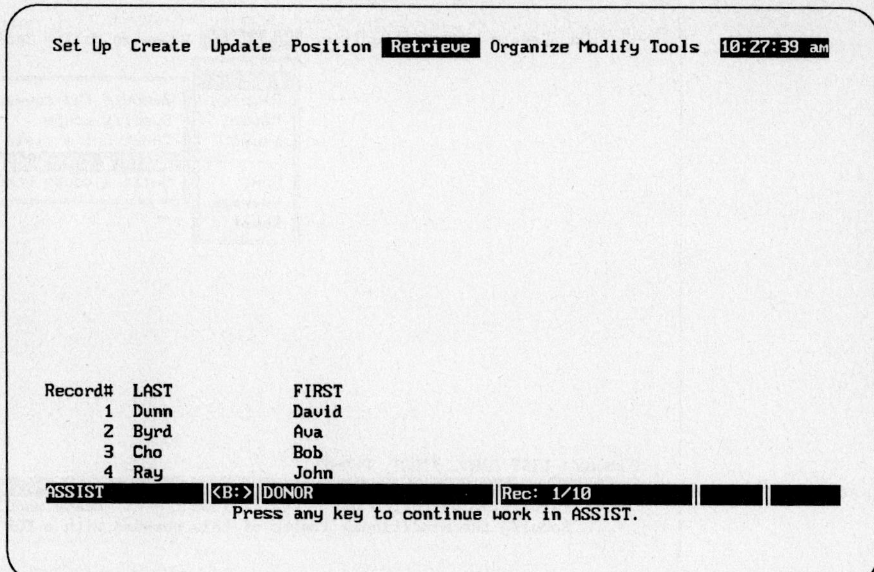

Figure 3.5 Retrieving a partial list of records.

Extras

If you do not remember what the structure of the database looks like, you can easily see it by choosing Tools and then moving the arrow to List structure and pressing the Enter key.

There are many more options you can learn with the ASSIST menu. For example, you might want to know how to insert new records, how to edit records, change record structure, and write reports. All these features can be done with ASSIST, but you will learn these new functions by using the powerful dBASE III PLUS command structure. You should be aware that anything you learned with ASSIST can easily be done utilizing the command structure, as you will see in the next chapter.

Quitting

Select SET UP. Quit dBase III Plus if you wish to quit now. If you are going on to the next lesson, do not quit.

On Your Own

Explain what the following selections will do:

1. Position, Goto Record, Record, 4
2. Position, Goto Record, Record, 19
3. Retrieve, Display, Specify scope, Record, 9, Execute the command, ENTER.
4. Retrieve, Display, Specify scope, Next, 3, Execute the command, ENTER.
5. List, Specify scope, Record, 2, Construct a field list, zip, touch right arrow, Execute the command, ENTER.

What selections are necessary for the following to be performed?

1. Position the pointer to record 4.

   (Position, Goto Record, Record, 4)
2. See the seventh record.

   (Retrieve, Display, Specify scope, Record, 7, Execute the command)
3. Go back to see the sixth record after seeing the seventh.

   (Retrieve, Display, Specify scope, Record, 6, Execute the command)
4. See records eight, nine, ten.

   (Retrieve, Display, Specify scope, Rest, Execute the command)
5. See the city and state for all donors.

(Retrieve, List, Construct a field list, CityState, touch right arrow, Execute the command, press Enter)

6. See the city and state for all donors 1 to 5. (Goto Top, Retrieve, Display, Specify scope, Next, 5, Construct a field list, CityState, touch right arrow, Execute the command)

On Your Own

[illegible]

4

Creating a New Database Structure

At the end of this chapter you should know how to

- **use the command structure to create a file.**

Important commands in this chapter:

- **.CREATE**
- **.GO TOP**
- **.LIST**

If you quit after the last lesson, start dBASE III PLUS as instructed in Chapter 2.

You are now going to create a file with the Command structure. As we said in the last chapter, you could have done this with the ASSIST, but there are clear advantages to using the command mode. First, there are more commands you can use in the command mode than in the ASSIST. It is quicker and easier to get dBASE to accomplish what you want by using commands. This should become obvious in the next two chapters.

If you are still in the ASSIST, leave it by pressing the Esc key. If you would like to return to the ASSIST, type **ASSIST**. *(All typing instructions will be shown in* ***bold*** *type, to indicate exactly what should be typed. For example, you just typed*

ASSIST only, not the period after the word.) You are now at the dot. (As mentioned in the preface, in this limited version of dBASE III PLUS the word DEMO in parentheses will always appear before the dot.) This is where you issue all commands. Assuming you see the DONOR file in use (look at the status line), type **LIST** and press the return key. Immediately you get a list of ten names from the donor list. The pointer is now at the end of the file. Type **GO TOP** and the pointer goes to the top of the file. Now type **CLEAR**. (Guess what this command does?)

1 Set the correct drive. If the command line does not show the correct drive, you will have to change it. (We will be putting our file on drive B.) Type **SET DEFAULT TO B** and press return. (If you want to put the files on drive A, type **SET DEFAULT TO A.**) dBASE lets you save time by allowing you to type only the first four letters of a command if you so wish. Thus, you could have typed **SET DEFA TO B**.

2 Type **CREATE**; then press the Enter key.

3 Name the file. Enter the name of the file you will be creating. Call it PLEDGES since it will relate to items pledged to the university (from Chapter 1).

4 Set up the structure of the file. You have done this before. Assume the fields will look like the following:

Field Name	Type	Width	Decimal
DNUM	Character	5	
PAIDUP	Logical	1	
DONORSINCE	Character	4	
DATECALLED	Date	8	
ITEMPROMIS	Character	10	
PURPOSE	Character	15	
VALUE	Numeric	7	2
INFORMAT	Memo	10	

To switch from character to numeric, date, logical, or memo, remember to press the space bar when type appears. After you enter the last field, press Enter two times.

Let us review and expand our discussion of the logical, date, numeric, and memo fields we encountered in Chapter 3. For the logical field, associate either a T or an F (true or false) or a Y or an N (yes or no) for this field. For example, either the person is a paid-up member or she is not. The width in the date field is automatically inserted to be 8 since it is of the form mm/dd/yy (note that the slash marks count as part of the field).

The numeric field stores numbers. If we assume a value will not exceed $9999.99, then a width of 7 is chosen. The decimal point counts as part of the field width. A dec of 2 means we are allowing two decimal places to the right of the period in the number. The memo field can hold large amounts of textual information. The memo field is automatically given a width of 10.

Now enter the records by answering Y.

Watch your capitals when entering data.

DNUM	PAIDUP	DONORSINCE	DATECALLED	ITEMPROMIS	PURPOSE	VALUE	INFORMAT
20	T	1978	10/03/87	Currency	Scholarship	25	Memo
32	F	1985	11/03/87	Stock	None	200	Memo
39	T	1986	11/14/87	Art	Gym	600	Memo
13	T	1985	11/03/87	Currency	Scholarship	15	Memo
91	F	1986	11/04/87	Computer	Education	1000	Memo
93	T	1977	11/04/87	Currency	Athletics	10	Memo
95	T	1983	10/03/87	Currency	Athletics	10	Memo
100	T	1985	10/03/87	Currency	None	10	Memo
102	T	1984	11/14/87	Currency	Scholarship	15	Memo
105	T	1985	11/14/87	Currency	Scholarship	100	Memo

When you are done, save the file by first holding down the Ctrl (control) key while at the same time pressing the End key.

What happens if you make an error when inputting data?

NOTE: If you made an error when typing, and if you did *not* press the return key, you can use the backspace key to delete the mistake. If you did press the return key, you can easily replace a letter by typing over it, or insert a character by pressing the Ins key (notice that Ins appears in the status bar on the right) and then typing the letter. (You can turn off the Ins option by pressing the Ins key one more time.)

Everything is pretty straightforward except for the memo field. To enter information, position the cursor in the memo field. Press the Ctrl key and then PgDn. Type in the text. When you are done, press Ctrl and then PgUp.

Let us put in the following INFORMAT for the DNUM 91, 95, 102, and 105 by paging up or down to the appropriate records:

For DNUM 91, type in: **Will give more next year**
For DNUM 95, type in: **Will be moving in March**
For DNUM 102, type in: **Lost job this year**
For DNUM 105, type in: **President of Acme Tools**

You can recall the records by entering EDIT at the prompt and then using PgUp/PgDn to find the record. If you do not want to continue with the next lesson now, save the file by holding down Ctrl while pressing End.

5

Looking at Information in a Database Using dBASE III Commands

At the end of this chapter you should know how to maneuver within a database.

Important commands in this chapter:

- **.COUNT**
- **.SUM**
- **.AVERAGE**
- **.DISPLAY ALL**
- **.QUIT**

If you saved your file in the previous lesson, you will need to enter USE PLEDGES and ENTER.

Now see how easy it is to enter some of the commands in dBASE. Type in the following.

Go Top— This command brings the pointer to the top of the file. You could have also typed **Goto Top.**

Skip 3— This command skips the pointer to record 4.

Skip –1— This command brings the pointer back one.

Goto Record 6— This brings the pointer to record 6. You could also type **Goto Reco 6.** Remember, you do not have to type all the letters of the record, just the first four letters. This is true for *any* command.

Goto Bottom— This command brings the pointer to the end of the file. You could have also typed it as **Goto Bott** or **Go Bott.**

Disp Reco 3— This command means to display record 3. Of course, it could have been typed as **Display Record 3.** To make the record even more presentable, that is, to get everything on one line, type **Disp Reco 3 off;** this removes the record number. The display looks better now.

List

TIP: If you press the up arrow at the prompt, dBASE will show you the last command that was entered. If you touch the arrow again dBASE will show you the command typed in before that one. This history feature is very useful if you want to repeat a recent command or if you need to do some editing. Try it to see the LIST one more time. Try it again, this time editing it by typing in the word **off** after list.

Go top; then **Disp Reco 5**— (Try this command with the history feature by pressing the up arrow a few times until you get Disp Reco 3 and then change it.) We now see record 5.

Go 7— The pointer is now at record 7.

Disp Reco 2

List Dnum, Value

List itempromis, VALUE— Notice that it makes no difference if you use capitals or lowercase when you list the fields.

List Itempromis, value, Informat

List for Value = 10 off— You get a list of everyone who gave $10.

List for Value > 20 off— You get a list of everyone who gave more than $20.

NOTE: There are six **relational operators** that come in handy: (1) =, (2) <> (means not equal), (3) > (means greater than, (4) = >= (means greater than or equal to), (5) < (means less than), (6) <= (means less than or equal to).

.List for purpose = "Scholarship"; then **List off for purpose = "Scholarship" off**— (to make the entry easier try using the history feature.)

You can search a field for a particular name. The name must be typed exactly as it appears in the field. If uppercase letters were used, then you have to put quotes around the word in uppercase. Try typing in the above with scholarship in caps: **List for purpose = "SCHOLARSHIP"**. You do not find any match.

NOTE: The quotes or delimiters are necessary when comparing character fields to literal characters.

Now type **List for purpose <> "Scholarship"**— You are now checking all those who gave items for any purpose excluding scholarship.

TIP: If you typed some words in caps and others in lowercase and would like to see them all at one time, type **List for upper(purpose) = "SCHOLARSHIP"** The word upper will allow all characters in the field to be treated as uppercase, even if they were not typed that way.

Type **.List for upper(itempromis) = "CURRENCY"**— This gives you all currency even though it was originally entered in lowercase!

Logical Operators

Many times you can find what you are after by using logical operators, which are of the form .NOT. , .AND., and .OR. There *must* be a period before and after the operator; the period tells dBASE it is a logical operator.

1. .NOT. tests if a condition is not true.
2. .AND. tests whether both conditions are true.
3. .OR. tests whether either condition is true or both are true.

If more than one logical operator is used, use parentheses to make the meaning clear; dBASE evaluates expressions in the order of (), .NOT., .AND., and .OR.

Try the use of the logical operators by typing the following:

List for .NOT. paidup— Here you want a list of all donors who are not paid up.

List for itempromis = "Art" .OR. itempromis = "Stock"— Here you want a list of all people who have donated art or stock to the university.

List for itempromis = "Currency" .AND. value = 10

List for itempromis = "Currency" .OR. value = 10

dBASE allows some useful mathematical calculations that can add more meaning to the data: COUNT, SUM, and AVERAGE.

COUNT

.Count for itempromis = "Currency" tells us how many people donated currency.

SUM

.Sum value informs you what the total amount pledged adds up to in dollars and cents. .Sum value for itempromis <> "Computer" gives you the total amount donated for everything except computers.

AVERAGE

.Average value gives you the average amount donated; other examples, .Average value for paidup; .Average value for .NOT. paidup.

DISPLAY

We have been using LIST quite often. Another useful command, similar to LIST, is DISPLAY, which displays the first twenty records on the screen and then waits for you to press any other key before it displays the next screenful. The LIST command, as you remember, shows you everything by scrolling across the screen without pausing. When the number of records exceeds twenty-four, the first few records on the screen might pass by too quickly. However, you can stop the display by holding down the Ctrl key and pressing the S key. When you want to continue, just press any key.

Try the following: **Display all;** then **Display for value > 10.**

Useful Commands

Several useful commands, some of which we have seen, can come in handy:

1. .DISPLAY— lets you see a particular record.
2. .GO <number> — when a number is inserted, the pointer will be positioned at a particular record.
3. .GO TOP— the pointer is now at the first record.
4. .GO BOTTOM— the pointer is now at the last record.
5. .LIST— you can see the whole database file with this command.
6. .Set default to <d>— when a letter such as A, B, or C is inserted for <d>, files will be assessed from and written to that drive.

7. .Use <d>:name of file— this command will open a database file in a particular drive, where d represents the drive.
8. .QUIT— this command lets you leave dBASE. *NEVER* shut down the computer when in dBASE without quitting, or you will lose data.

Leave dBASE by using QUIT.

On Your Own

1. List off
2. List informat
3. List paidup, Informat
4. List for value >100
5. List for itempromis "currency"
6. List for itempromis "currency"
7. List for .NOT. paidup .AND. purpose = "education"
8. List for UPPER(purpose) = "NONE"
9. List for purpose = "a"
10. Display for value >99 .and. value <2000

NOTE: Remember to use QUIT.

6

Adding Records to a File

At the end of this chapter you should know how to

- **update records.**

Important command in this chapter:

- **.APPEND**

Typically, you will need to add new records to your database file. Naturally, you want to keep all records up to date. In the DONOR file, for example, the university is constantly calling potential donors, so you need to keep these people on file. An easy way to do this is with the command APPEND. (In future chapters, you will see how to delete and edit records as well.) The procedure is as follows:

1. Choose the database file you wish to add to.

   Start off by checking the status bar to make sure you are in the correct drive. If you are not in the correct drive, type **SET DEFAULT TO** drive used. Now type in **USE DONOR**. Notice that DONOR is displayed in the command bar.

2. Type **APPEND**. This command enables you to add records.

3. Enter the record. The screen looks similar to the way it was when new data was being inputted in the CREATE mode. The status bar will now show APPEND on the left. Record EOF/10 appears on the right as a reminder that

presently there are ten records and you will be inputting record 11. A new record is always added to the bottom of the file. (You'll see in Chapter10 how you can insert a record anywhere you wish.)

Assume you have the following record to add: DNUM:94. The name of the person is Alan Stone. He lives at 4 Park Lane in Newton, Mass. His Zip code is 02163, and his telephone number is 617–566–3811.

When the record has been properly entered, hold down Ctrl and press End. Check that the record is there by typing **.LIST**

On Your Own

Add the following record to the PLEDGES file: DNUM:94. He is a paid-up individual. He has been a donor since 1985. He was called 1/5/88 and pledged a computer valued at $1900. He would like to give the computer for the purpose of education. He also told you that two more computers will be donated next year.

Save all your work by issuing the command QUIT.

7

Changing the Way the Database Looks

At the end of this chapter you should know how to

- **modify the structure of a database file.**

Important command in this chapter:

- **.MODIFY STRUCTURE**

One of the most common problems you may encounter when learning dBASE is that you misjudged the width of one or more fields. Typically, you would like to make the field width larger. For example, a width of 10 characters may have been set for a field called LASTNAME. One individual may have a last name of 11 letters, and you discover this only after 171 records have already been entered. What do you do? Start over again? No; the answer is to reshape the structure of the database.

Another potential problem occurs when a field name is forgotten initially or you later feel that adding another field would make the database more complete and useful. Finally, still another potential problem occurs if want to change the name of a field.

Restart dBASE and set default to your data save drive.

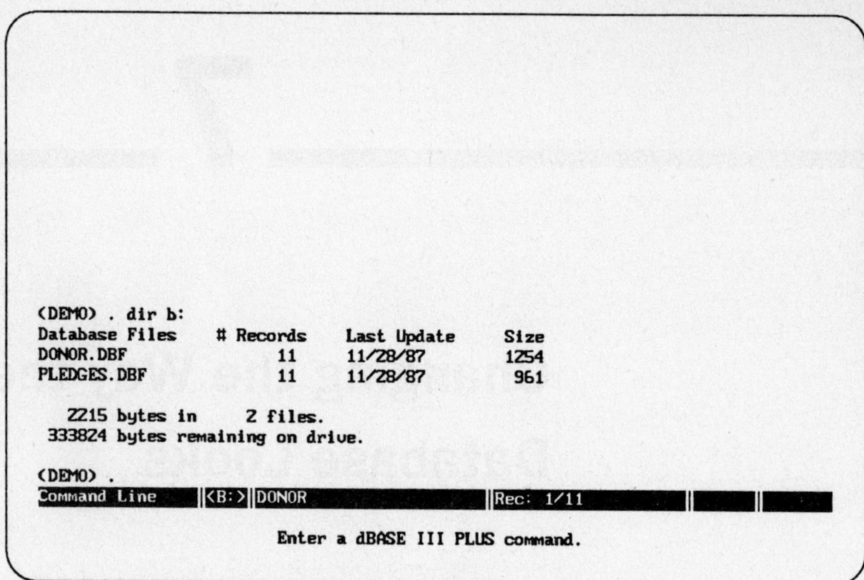

(DEMO) . dir b:
Database Files # Records Last Update Size
DONOR.DBF 11 11/28/87 1254
PLEDGES.DBF 11 11/28/87 961
2215 bytes in 2 files.
333824 bytes remaining on drive.
(DEMO) .
Command Line <B:> DONOR Rec: 1/11
Enter a dBASE III PLUS command.

Figure 7.1 Database files stored on the disk.

Before you change the structure, see what database files are stored on your disk. Be sure your default is displayed in the command bar <A:> or <B:>. Type **DIR**; notice that unlike when you type this in DOS, you get only database files.

In Figure 7.1, you see the names of the database files, how many records are in each file, when the file was last updated, and the size of the file. You can also see how many total bytes are in the files on your disk and how many bytes still remain on the disk. For small files, there is never a problem of using up the bytes on the disk, but you should check this point when your file becomes large.

Select your data drive by typing **SET DEFAULT TO** data drive. You will be using the file PLEDGES. Type **USE PLEDGES**; this command opens the file.

Before you make any change to the structure of the file, first see what the file looks like. Type the command: **DISPLAY STRUCTURE**. (See Figure 7.2.)

Besides the structure of the database, you can see how many records are in your file and when the file was last updated. The total number of bytes in the fields is also totaled. Note that it shows 61 bytes, although when we add it up it is only 60. The discrepancy occurs because dBASE adds one position

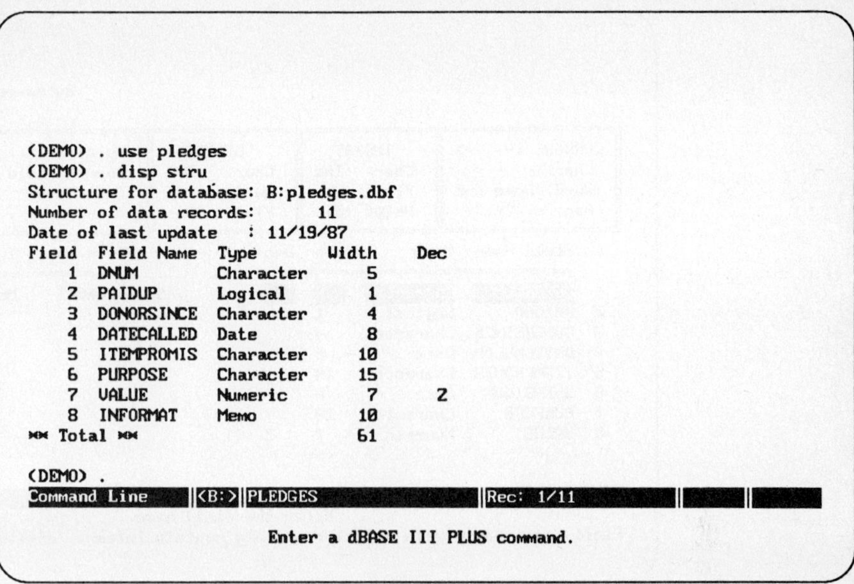
(DEMO) . use pledges
(DEMO) . disp stru
Structure for database: B:pledges.dbf
Number of data records: 11
Date of last update : 11/19/87
Field Field Name Type Width Dec
1 DNUM Character 5
2 PAIDUP Logical 1
3 DONORSINCE Character 4
4 DATECALLED Date 8
5 ITEMPROMIS Character 10
6 PURPOSE Character 15
7 VALUE Numeric 7 2
8 INFORMAT Memo 10
** Total ** 61
(DEMO) .
Command Line
<B:>
PLEDGES
Rec: 1/11
Enter a dBASE III PLUS command.

Figure 7.2 Structure of the PLEDGES file.

for use when a record is deleted. It inserts a star (*) in that position, which is reserved.

Type **MODIFY STRUCTURE**. This screen looks similar to the one for inputting data except MODIFY STRUCTURE appears in the status line. Now try three different examples.

Example 1: Changing the field name from one name to another. We decide the name DONORNUM seems easier to remember than DNUM.

1. Type the new name and press Ctrl and then End.
2. Answer Y to the question, "Should data be copied from backup for all fields?" (dBASE creates temporary files besides the .database file (dbf), and these must be updated as well.) Press Enter.
3. Check out the result by typing **LIST**.

Example 2: Changing a field length. Say you would like to change the field width in the field PURPOSE from 15 to 20.

1. Type **Modify Structure**. Bring the cursor down to the width, which now says 15.
2. Type in 20 and press the Enter key.

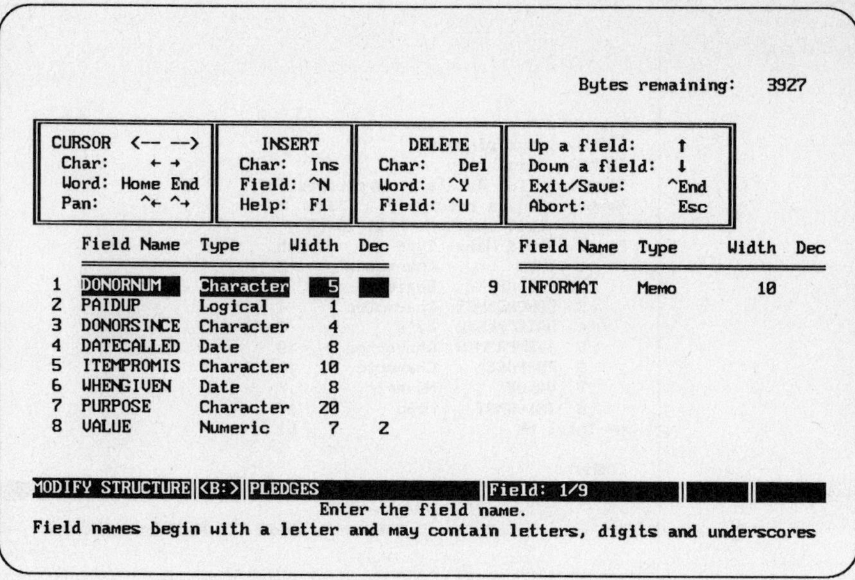

Figure 7.3 Result of adding a new field.

3 Holding down the Ctrl key, press the End key. Press Enter.

Example 3: Adding a new field. In the PLEDGE file, you now want to keep a record of when the pledge was given. You will insert this record after the field ITEMPROMIS.

1 Type **Modify Structure**. Position the cursor on field 6 (which is PURPOSE).

2 Holding down the Ctrl key, press N. Note on the screen information that tells you which keys to press for inserting and deleting and other key movements as well.

3 Type **WHENGIVEN** and make it a date field. See Figure 7.3. Holding down the Ctrl key, press the End key. Press Enter.

On Your Own

1. Change the field width in VALUE from 7 to 9.
2. Reverse what you did in exercise 1.
3. Remove the field WHENGIVEN from the PLEDGES file.

4. Change the field length PURPOSE, in the PLEDGES file, back to 15. QUIT if you are not going on to the next lesson at this time.

8

Updating and Removing Records

At the end of this chapter you should know how to

- **browse through a database.**
- **replace selected information in fields.**
- **delete records.**

Important commands in this chapter:

- **.EDIT**
- **.BROWSE**
- **.REPLACE**
- **.DELETE**
- **.RECALL**
- **.ERASE**
- **.ZAP**

Editing

Occasionally you will have to remove records from your database for various reasons. A person may die, or a person may not want to receive any more calls from the university for donations. A person who was not a paid-up member may now become paid up, and we would like to reflect this new information in the database. Possibly the item you called currency should be called, more appropriately, money. You might have made an error a few months ago and just now noticed it.

You can make all these changes quickly and efficiently by updating your data. You will not change the structure as you did in the last chapter, only replace or delete data.

Start dBASE and set the default drive.

Begin by using the PLEDGES file (type **Use Pledges**) and assume DNUM 91 has paid up his membership. We are not sure which record he is. Type **LIST**. You see that you need to change record number 5, so type **EDIT 5**. All you need to do is bring the cursor to the appropriate field and type in a T for the F. Holding down the Ctrl key, press the End key. The file is now updated to reflect paid-up.

NOTE: If you touch the Esc key during editing, your changes will not be recorded.

Browsing

dBASE makes it easier for you to update a record by using the command .BROWSE. This command is useful when there is a relatively short database and you do not know the exact record number you wish to change. The command lets you edit, add records, and delete records very neatly. Type **GO TOP** to bring the pointer to the top and then type **BROWSE**.

To see beyond the 80 columns that the screen allots us, hold down the Ctrl key and touch the right arrow. (See the menu for a more complete listing of options that can be utilized with BROWSE command.) Press ESC.

You can use the BROWSE command to view selected fields as well. Type **BROWSE FIELDS DNUM, ITEMPROMIS**. Press Esc. If you do not want to see the menu on the screen while you are browsing, after pressing Escape, just type **SET MENU OFF**. Then type **BROWSE**.

To put the menu back on, after pressing Escape, type **SET MENU ON**. Then type **BROWSE**. You can now go through each record a field at a time by pressing the Enter key. Changes can then be made in that field. (Do not forget the Del (delete) and Ins keys can be used as well.) Try this out by changing VALUE in DNUM 95 to $5. Press Ctrl and End to save it.

If a record is to be added, bring the cursor down to the last record and press Enter. Answer Y to the prompt ADD NEW RECORDS and press Enter.

Likewise, you can delete a field or a record at the appropriate location by pressing Ctrl and then U.

The BROWSE command provides additional help when you press Ctrl and Home. On the top of the screen you see Bottom, Top, Lock, Record No., and Freeze. Bottom brings you to the end of the records; Top brings you to the top of the file.

Lock makes the leftmost columns remain in position when the screen moves to the right or left. Freeze places the cursor on a particular field. This is useful when you make changes to numerous records in one field. When you are done, hold down Ctrl and press End.

Replacing

After you created the file DONOR, you may have decided you wanted all the occurrences of the cities and states in complete uppercase. dBASE gives you an easy way to do this global updating, using the command REPLACE. You can change all the records to reflect this change. There is no need to use the BROWSE command to change each record individually. Bring in the DONOR file (type **Use Donor**) and type **LIST**. To change all the cities and states to caps, type **REPLACE ALL CITYSTATE WITH UPPER(CITYSTATE).**

If DNUM were a numeric field and you decided to change all the donor numbers by adding 100 to each of them, you *could* accomplish this by typing **REPLACE ALL DNUM WITH DNUM+100.** DNUM is not a numeric so don't attempt this.

Deleting and Recalling

Deleting records is easy. List the file and type **DELETE RECORD 5.** This command deleted record 5 from the database. Type **LIST OFF** (see Figure 8.1). You see the same file, except that there is a star in front of the first field by record 5 (that is, record 93). What is going on?

The DELETE command works this way. After a record has been "supposedly" deleted, you have three options:

1. See the database file as before, except that this deleted record is starred (that is what you chose).
2. Recall the "deleted" record by undeleting it; the star will then disappear.
3. Permanently delete it.

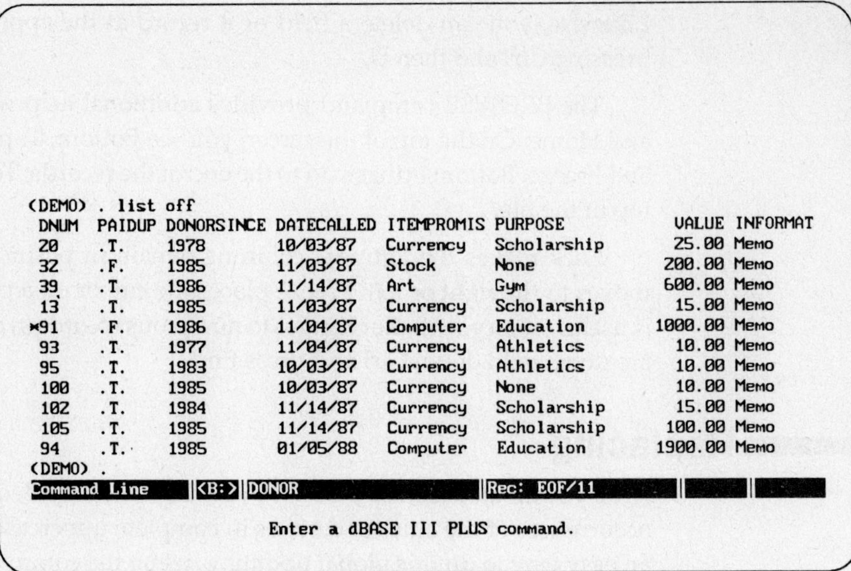
```
(DEMO) . list off
 DNUM  PAIDUP DONORSINCE DATECALLED ITEMPROMIS PURPOSE              VALUE INFORMAT
 20    .T.    1978       10/03/87   Currency   Scholarship          25.00 Memo
 32    .F.    1985       11/03/87   Stock      None                200.00 Memo
 39    .T.    1986       11/14/87   Art        Gym                 600.00 Memo
 13    .T.    1985       11/03/87   Currency   Scholarship          15.00 Memo
*91    .F.    1986       11/04/87   Computer   Education          1000.00 Memo
 93    .T.    1977       11/04/87   Currency   Athletics            10.00 Memo
 95    .T.    1983       10/03/87   Currency   Athletics            10.00 Memo
 100   .T.    1985       10/03/87   Currency   None                 10.00 Memo
 102   .T.    1984       11/14/87   Currency   Scholarship          15.00 Memo
 105   .T.    1985       11/14/87   Currency   Scholarship         100.00 Memo
 94    .T.    1985       01/05/88   Computer   Education          1900.00 Memo
(DEMO) .
Command Line   <B:> DONOR          Rec: EOF/11

              Enter a dBASE III PLUS command.
```

Figure 8.1 File with one record deleted.

Option 1

You chose option 1 and saw an asterisk before the first field, which is a reminder that this is a record which has been flagged for deletion. (If a list or display is typed you will always see the record.)

If you would like to retain the record for deletion but not see it on the screen, type **.SET DELETE ON**. This command permits the record to stay in the database but it will not be displayed on the screen. The only way to see the record is specifically to request the deleted record number (for example, .display reco 5).

You can use DELETE in other ways. Type **DELETE FOR LAST = "R"**. You might do this if you felt the typist inputting the names might have erred with all those names beginning with "R." All last names beginning with R will be flagged for deletion.

Retrieve the PLEDGES file and type **DELETE FOR VALUE < 15**. This deletes all records in which an individual had given less than a $15 gift.

NOTE: If you would like a list of only those records that have been deleted, we can type **LIST FOR DELETED()**. Before doing this be sure you type SET

DELETE OFF. This command will give you a list of all those records that have been starred.

If you wish to delete all the records, type **DELETE ALL**. Do it.

Option 2

If you wish to reinstate a record or a group of records (maybe you have changed your mind about deleting), you can do so easily. Suppose the university would like again to keep on file those individuals who gave money regardless of how much they donated. Type **RECALL FOR VALUE > 10**.

Or suppose the typist who input all the last names beginning with the letter R really did it correctly. After bringing in the DONOR file, type **RECALL FOR LAST = "R"**. If you wish you can recall all the records by typing **RECALL ALL**.

Option 3

This option "really" removes the records permanently from the file. All you need to do is type the command PACK. This command removes the records that were marked for deletion and repacks the remaining records. Use this command with care! RECALL can *not* now bring the records back.

Erasing

There are two other ways to delete records: .ZAP and .ERASE. .ZAP removes all records from the database, whether or not they are marked for deletion. When the command is given, all records are lost. Only the structure of the database remains. Be careful before using .ZAP! .ERASE <filename> removes a file from a disk directory. Be careful before using it!

On Your Own

1. Edit record 5 in the file PLEDGES and replace PAIDUP with F.
2. Change DNUM to a numeric field and add 100 to each DNUM.
3. Recall all the deleted records in the file PLEDGES.
4. Subtract 100 from each record in the field DNUM and change DNUM to a character field.

5. Change the field VALUE of DNUM 95 back to $10.
6. Remove donor number 94 from the PLEDGES file.
7. Remove Alan Stone from the DONOR file.

If you are not going on to the next lesson at this time be sure to QUIT.

9

Rearranging Data

At the end of this chapter you should know how to

- **sort a database**
- **index on a database**
- **reindex a database**

Important commands in this chapter:

- **.SORT**
- **.INDEX**
- **.REINDEX**

Sorting

Sorting on a database file can be quite useful. Sorting is just rearranging the data in a more meaningful manner. For example, you may want to send out a mailing list with Zip codes in ascending order, or you may just want a list of values of the donations in descending order. Often, all you need is a list of names printed in alphabetical order. You can use one of two commands to enable you to do this:

.SORT TO <FILENAME> ON <FIELD>
.SORT ON <FIELD> TO <FILENAME>

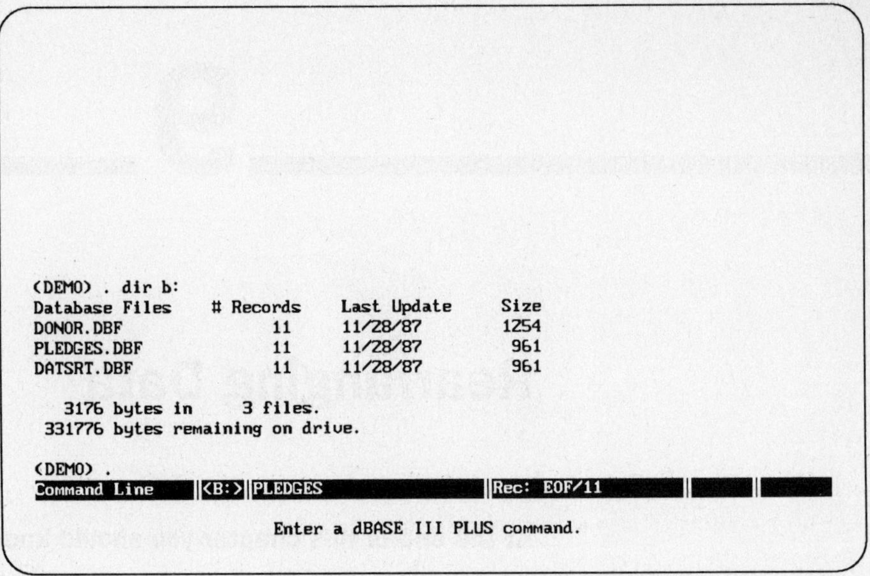

(DEMO) . dir b:
Database Files # Records Last Update Size
DONOR.DBF 11 11/28/87 1254
PLEDGES.DBF 11 11/28/87 961
DATSRT.DBF 11 11/28/87 961
3176 bytes in 3 files.
331776 bytes remaining on drive.
(DEMO) .
Command Line
<B:>
PLEDGES
Rec: EOF/11
Enter a dBASE III PLUS command.

Figure 9.1 Illustrating that the PLEDGES and DATSRT files are identical in size.

The filename is the new name under which the sorted records are saved. The field is the character, numeric, or date field which you want to sort. The procedure is:

1 Start dBASE III and set default drive. Then type **DIR;** then **USE PLEDGES;** and finally, **LIST** (just to see it).

2 Use the SORT command on the field you wish to sort and name the new sorted file. Type **SORT ON DATECALLED TO DATSRT**. In the above example, you wish to get a sorted file of PLEDGES sorted by the date people were called. Call this new file DATSRT.

You have just created a new file identical in bytes to the first one, except this file is sorted chronologically by date (see Figure 9.1). This new file will take up room on your disk. The first file, PLEDGES, does not change at all. To see this, type **dir**.

Check the structure of each file by typing **.List structure** and notice that they are both the same (see Figure 9.2). To see the structure of the second file DATSRT, type **Use datsrt**; then type **.List structure.**

3 See the sorted file. Type **USE DATSRT**; then type **.LIST**.

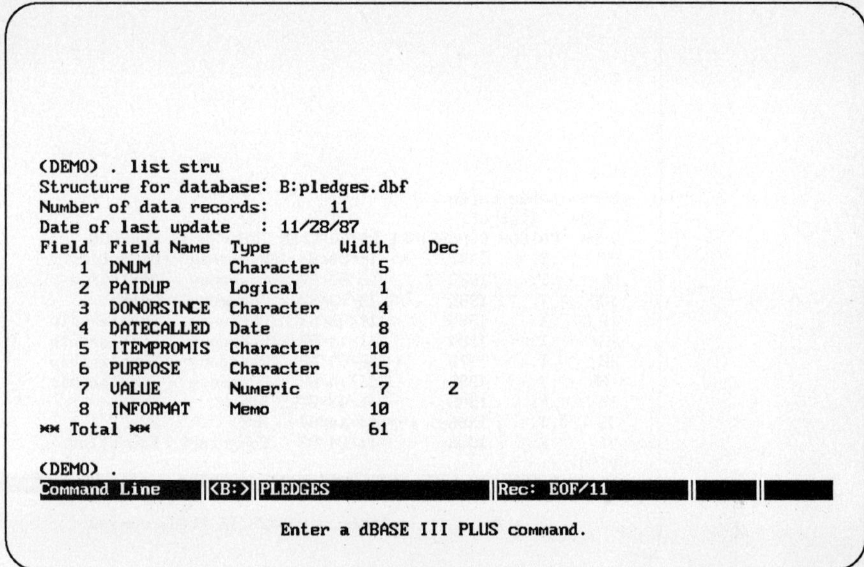

```
(DEMO) . list stru
Structure for database: B:pledges.dbf
Number of data records:      11
Date of last update   : 11/28/87
Field  Field Name  Type       Width    Dec
    1  DNUM        Character      5
    2  PAIDUP      Logical        1
    3  DONORSINCE  Character      4
    4  DATECALLED  Date           8
    5  ITEMPROMIS  Character     10
    6  PURPOSE     Character     15
    7  VALUE       Numeric        7      2
    8  INFORMAT    Memo          10
** Total **                      61

(DEMO) .
Command Line  |<B:>|PLEDGES          |Rec: EOF/11
                  Enter a dBASE III PLUS command.
```

Figure 9.2a Structure for PLEDGES file.

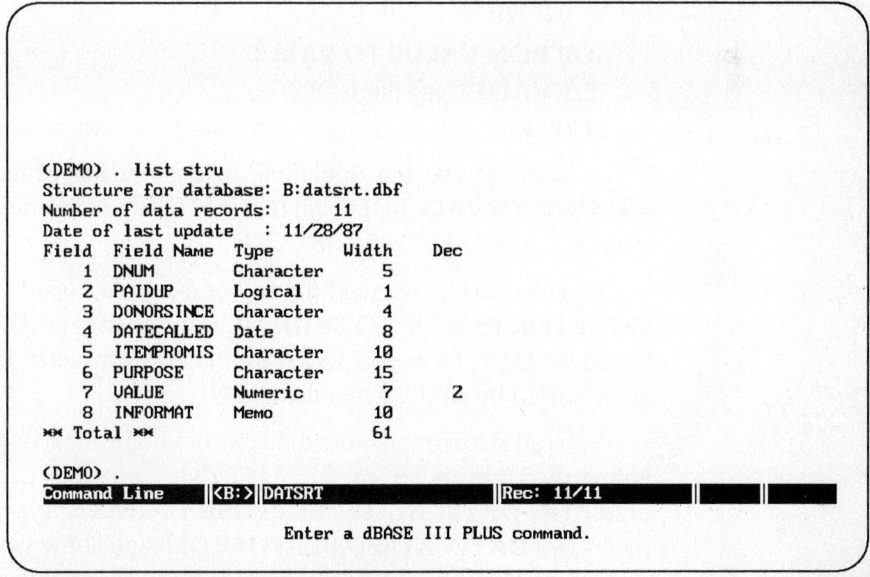

```
(DEMO) . list stru
Structure for database: B:datsrt.dbf
Number of data records:      11
Date of last update   : 11/28/87
Field  Field Name  Type       Width    Dec
    1  DNUM        Character      5
    2  PAIDUP      Logical        1
    3  DONORSINCE  Character      4
    4  DATECALLED  Date           8
    5  ITEMPROMIS  Character     10
    6  PURPOSE     Character     15
    7  VALUE       Numeric        7      2
    8  INFORMAT    Memo          10
** Total **                      61

(DEMO) .
Command Line  |<B:>|DATSRT           |Rec: 11/11
                  Enter a dBASE III PLUS command.
```

Figure 9.2b Structure for DATSRT file.

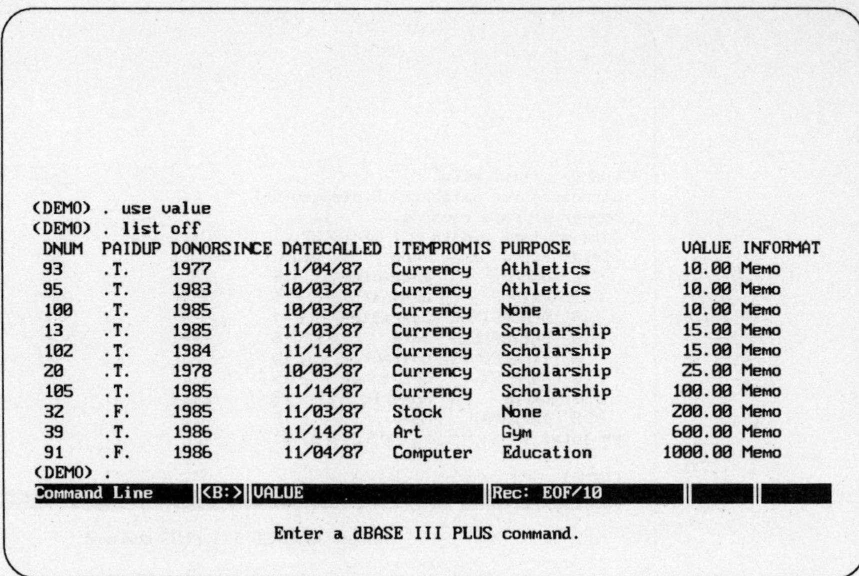

```
(DEMO) . use value
(DEMO) . list off
 DNUM  PAIDUP DONORSINCE DATECALLED ITEMPROMIS PURPOSE          VALUE INFORMAT
 93    .T.     1977      11/04/87   Currency   Athletics        10.00 Memo
 95    .T.     1983      10/03/87   Currency   Athletics        10.00 Memo
 100   .T.     1985      10/03/87   Currency   None             10.00 Memo
 13    .T.     1985      11/03/87   Currency   Scholarship      15.00 Memo
 102   .T.     1984      11/14/87   Currency   Scholarship      15.00 Memo
 20    .T.     1978      10/03/87   Currency   Scholarship      25.00 Memo
 105   .T.     1985      11/14/87   Currency   Scholarship     100.00 Memo
 32    .F.     1985      11/03/87   Stock      None            200.00 Memo
 39    .T.     1986      11/14/87   Art        Gym             600.00 Memo
 91    .F.     1986      11/04/87   Computer   Education      1000.00 Memo
(DEMO) .
Command Line    ||<B:>||VALUE            ||Rec: EOF/10       ||    ||

                  Enter a dBASE III PLUS command.
```

Figure 9.3 PLEDGES file sorted on VALUE.

Here are some examples. You could see the donations given to the university by typing

SORT ON VALUE TO VALUE
USE VALUE (see Figure 9.3)
LIST OFF

If you want to see the donations in descending order, type **SORT ON VALUE/D TO VALUEDES.** All that was needed was the /D. Look at the difference. Use **VALUEDES; LIST OFF.**

You can sort on selected fields. For example, type **SORT ON DONORSINCE FOR PAIDUP TO PAIDSORT** and then type **.USE PAIDSORT** followed by **LIST**. Here you will see a listing from when the donors had first given sorted by paid-up members only.

You can also sort on more than one field. The most important field should be specified first and the remaining fields separated by commas. For example, **SORT ON DATECALLED, PURPOSE TO DATE**. Typing **USE DATE** and then **LIST DATECALLED,PURPOSE OFF** will show you the file PLEDGES sorted in order of purpose within the date called and the sorted records stored in the file DATE. You can see that on 10/03/87 three calls were made. The field ATHLETICS comes before NONE, which comes before SCHOLARSHIP.

On Your Own

Do all these exercises with the file PLEDGES.

1. .SORT ON DONORSINCE TO HISTORY
2. .SORT TO PURPOSE TO PURPOSE (use field PURPOSE)
3. .SORT TO DATESRT ON DATE CALLED
4. .SORT ON DONORSINCE FOR .NOT. PAIDUP TO NTPDSORT
5. .SORT ON ITEMPROMIS TO ITEM FOR VALUE > 25
6. Type DIR to see all the files you've created.

Indexing

You saw that each time you performed another sort you got an identical file as far as number of bytes occupied. This begins to add up to many bytes as you do more sorts. At present the file is pretty small. However, if you add more records, you will notice sorting taking a much longer time. An unforseen problem occurs when a record is added to a sorted file. The record does not go automatically to the right slot; it gets appended to the end. You would have to sort the records again to get every record in the right place. Fortunately, dBASE III provides a solution via **indexing**, which can help reduce the first two problems and eliminate the problem you get with APPEND. Indexing automatically updates changes made to the database.

NOTE: The only thing indexing cannot do that sort can is have character or date fields in descending order. It can, however, put numeric fields in descending order.

Index, unlike sort, does not create another database file; it creates an index file that is smaller.

The procedure is as follows:

1. Select the file you want to index. Type **USE DONOR**.
2. Type the INDEX command. The format for the command is .INDEX ON <filename> TO <new filename>. Type **INDEX ON LAST TO LASTNAME.** To see what you have done, type **LIST LAST, FIRST, CITYSTATE.** (See Figure 9.4.)

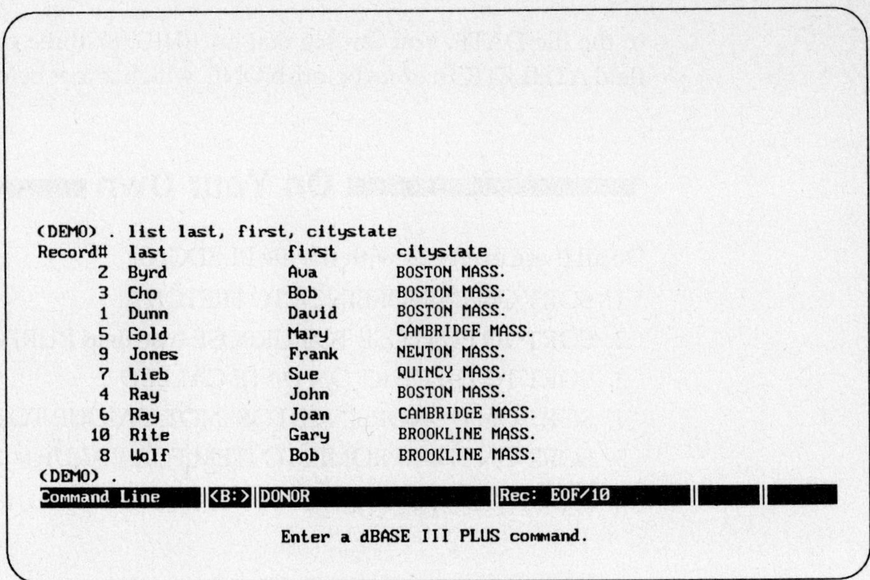

```
(DEMO) . list last, first, citystate
Record#  last          first        citystate
      2  Byrd          Ava          BOSTON MASS.
      3  Cho           Bob          BOSTON MASS.
      1  Dunn          David        BOSTON MASS.
      5  Gold          Mary         CAMBRIDGE MASS.
      9  Jones         Frank        NEWTON MASS.
      7  Lieb          Sue          QUINCY MASS.
      4  Ray           John         BOSTON MASS.
      6  Ray           Joan         CAMBRIDGE MASS.
     10  Rite          Gary         BROOKLINE MASS.
      8  Wolf          Bob          BROOKLINE MASS.
(DEMO) .
Command Line  ||<B:>||DONOR            ||Rec: EOF/10  ||   ||
                      Enter a dBASE III PLUS command.
```

Figure 9.4 DONOR file indexed on LASTNAME.

Create another index: Type **INDEX ON CITYSTATE TO LOCATION** and then **LIST LAST, FIRST, CITYSTATE.** (See Figure 9.5.)

Create still another index: Type **INDEX ON FIRST TO FIRSTNAME** and then **LIST LAST, FIRST, CITYSTATE.** (See Figure 9.6.)

If you wish to make a previous index file active (for example, LASTNAME), you must open the index file. This is done by first typing **SET INDEX TO <index filename>**. Now type **SET INDEX TO LASTNAME** and **LIST LAST, FIRST, CITYSTATE.**

NOTE: You could open more than one indexed file by typing **SET INDEX TO <index file #1>, <index file #2>**, and so on.

Any change you make to the database file will be reflected in the index file only if it is open. If you type **SET INDEX TO LASTNAME, FIRSTNAME,** both files are open. Any change made to LASTNAME (which is the active file since it is listed first and there can only be one active file) will be reflected in FIRSTNAME as well.

NOTE: If you forgot to open all index files that you want to be updated, all you need to do when you remember is to type **SET INDEX TO <FILENAME>**, where <FILENAME> is the specific file you now wish updated. Now type **REINDEX.**

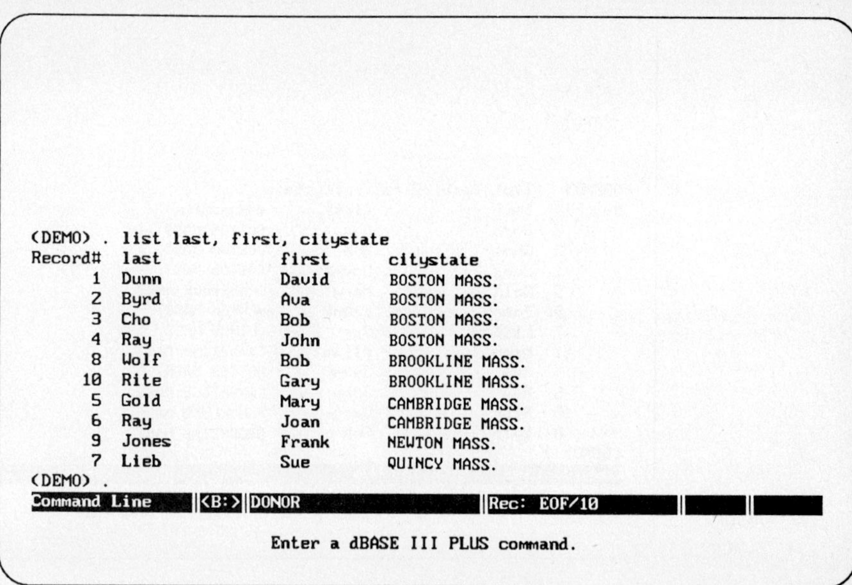

```
(DEMO) . list last, first, citystate
Record#  last          first      citystate
      1  Dunn          David      BOSTON MASS.
      2  Byrd          Ava        BOSTON MASS.
      3  Cho           Bob        BOSTON MASS.
      4  Ray           John       BOSTON MASS.
      8  Wolf          Bob        BROOKLINE MASS.
     10  Rite          Gary       BROOKLINE MASS.
      5  Gold          Mary       CAMBRIDGE MASS.
      6  Ray           Joan       CAMBRIDGE MASS.
      9  Jones         Frank      NEWTON MASS.
      7  Lieb          Sue        QUINCY MASS.
(DEMO) .
Command Line  |<B:>|DONOR          |Rec: EOF/10 | |

              Enter a dBASE III PLUS command.
```

Figure 9.5 DONOR file indexed on CITYSTATE.

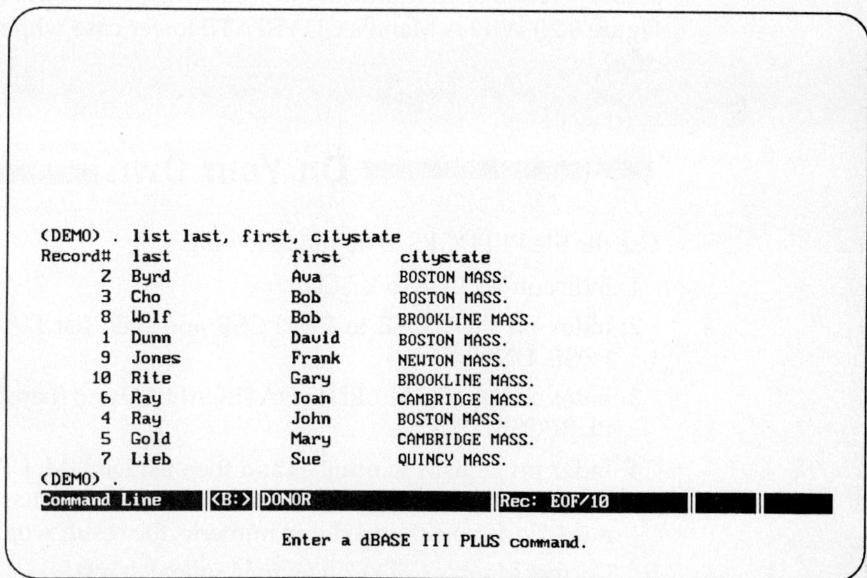

```
(DEMO) . list last, first, citystate
Record#  last          first      citystate
      2  Byrd          Ava        BOSTON MASS.
      3  Cho           Bob        BOSTON MASS.
      8  Wolf          Bob        BROOKLINE MASS.
      1  Dunn          David      BOSTON MASS.
      9  Jones         Frank      NEWTON MASS.
     10  Rite          Gary       BROOKLINE MASS.
      6  Ray           Joan       CAMBRIDGE MASS.
      4  Ray           John       BOSTON MASS.
      5  Gold          Mary       CAMBRIDGE MASS.
      7  Lieb          Sue        QUINCY MASS.
(DEMO) .
Command Line  |<B:>|DONOR          |Rec: EOF/10 | |

              Enter a dBASE III PLUS command.
```

Figure 9.6 DONOR file indexed on FIRSTNAME.

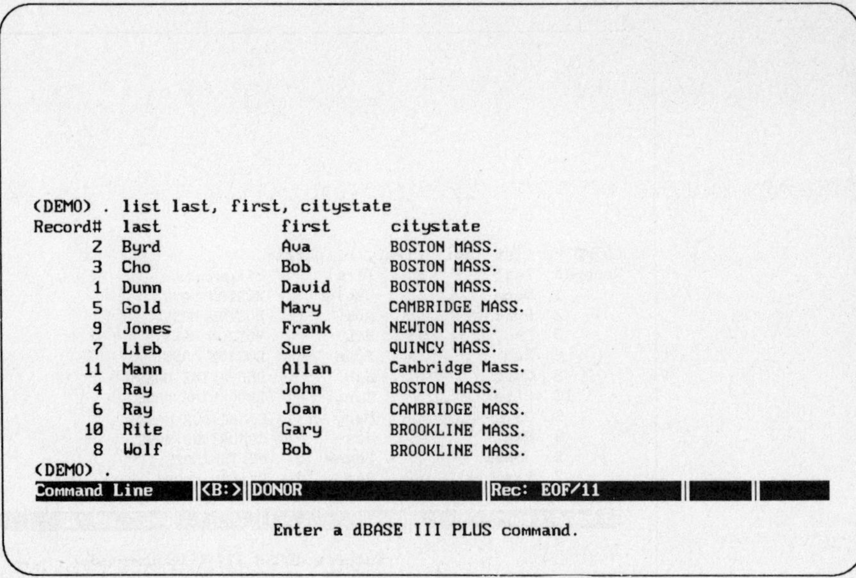
(DEMO) . list last, first, citystate
Record# last first citystate
2 Byrd Ava BOSTON MASS.
3 Cho Bob BOSTON MASS.
1 Dunn David BOSTON MASS.
5 Gold Mary CAMBRIDGE MASS.
9 Jones Frank NEWTON MASS.
7 Lieb Sue QUINCY MASS.
11 Mann Allan Cambridge Mass.
4 Ray John BOSTON MASS.
6 Ray Joan CAMBRIDGE MASS.
10 Rite Gary BROOKLINE MASS.
8 Wolf Bob BROOKLINE MASS.
(DEMO) .
Command Line <B:> DONOR Rec: EOF/11
Enter a dBASE III PLUS command.

Figure 9.7 The name Allan Mann added to DONOR file.

Now add a record to your file. The new record is DNUM 190. The name is Allan Mann; he lives at 2 Water Street Cambridge Mass. 02138, and his telephone number is 6175652547. Type **APPEND** and add the information. Then type **Ctrl End** to record it. Type **.LIST LAST, FIRST, CITYSTATE** to see how it has been updated. Notice the name is in the right position. (See Figure 9.7.) Why is Mann's CITYSTATE lower case while the rest are upper case?

On Your Own

Use the file PLEDGES to do the following:

1. Index on VALUE to VALUE.
2. Index on PURPOSE to PURPOSE and then list DATECALLED, PURPOSE, DNUM.
3. Index on DATECALLED to DATECALLED and then list DATECALLED, PURPOSE, DNUM.
4. Index on DNUM to number and then list DNUM, DATECALLED. (The reason for the strange result is that DNUM is a character field and not numeric. If you changed it to numeric, the result would be as expected.)
5. Correct Mann's CITYSTATE field to match rest.

QUIT if you're not going on to the next lesson.

10

Searching

At the end of this chapter you should know how to

- **search for specific information in a large database quickly.**

Important command in this chapter:

- **.SEEK**

Start dBASE and set the default drive.

With our small database file it is pretty easy to find a record. However, when a database file becomes large, it gets more difficult to zero in on the record you want quickly. dBASE III provides a command that can be used only on an index file to help you obtain information quickly. The command is .SEEK <expression>. For example, if you were using the file DONOR and had on the index LAST (that is, you first typed **.use donor** and then **.index on last to last**), you could then find a donor by the name of Gold by typing **.SEEK "Gold"**. You can then see it by typing **.DISP LAST, FIRST**.

NOTE: If you did not know the exact spelling of the name (only that it began with a "G"), you could type **SEEK "G"** and you would see the first of the last names that begin with the letter G. (If there is another one, and you want to see it, type **skip** and then **display**.)

NOTE: The data you are looking for must be in the field on which the index is presently active. So, if you had typed **SEEK "52"**, you would not have found it since you are not indexed on that field (you would have to type, for example, **index on dnum to dnum**).

Rules

1. .SEEK is case-sensitive. If you want to find "Gold," do not type "gold"; it will show No find.
2. Literal data must be enclosed in quotes (for example, **SEEK "Gold"** must be typed, not .SEEK .Gold).
3. To seek on a date, you must type **SEEK CTOD** ("the date desired").

On Your Own

Use the file PLEDGES to do the following:

1. INDEX on ITEMPROMIS to ITEMPROMIS

   .SEEK "Computer"

   .DISPLAY
2. SEEK "C"

   .DISP DNUM, PURPOSE
3. SET INDEX TO DATECALLED

   .SEEK CTOD ("11/04/87")

   .DISP
4. INDEX TO DONORSINCE TO DONORSINCE

   .SEEK "1984"

   .DISPLAY

An alternate command to use for finding a particular record when a file is not indexed is LOCATE. This command searches a database sequentially for a particular record. Let us use the DONOR file. For example, if you wish to find the name Gold, type **LOCATE FOR LAST = "Gold"**. You could see those people with last name beginning with "B" by typing **LOCATE FOR LAST = "B"**.

Try this one:

.GO 1
.LOCATE NEXT 2 for CITYSTATE = "B"

.CONTINUE
.CONTINUE

Try this:

.LOCATE FOR ZIP > "02170" .and. ZIP < "02175"

When would you use .LOCATE and when would you use .SEEK? .SEEK cannot be used unless the file is indexed. .LOCATE is generally slower than .SEEK since records are searched from the beginning.

Both commands are useful not only for finding a record but for editing. For example, if you want to edit a particular record (say "Gold," for example) and you do not know its record number, type **LOCATE "Gold"** and then type **edit**.

Be sure to QUIT if you are not going to do the next lesson now.

11

Generating Reports

At the end of this chapter you should know how to

- **design and write a report.**

Important commands in this chapter:

- **.REPORT FORM**
- **.MODIFY REPORT**

Start dBASE and set the default drive.

You can obtain printed reports with dBASE. You can provide titles, margins, page numbers, totals, and subtotals; you can save these reports on a disk and have them available anytime you wish.

Here you are going to design a report using the file PLEDGES. You want the report to list the donor numbers, the item promised, and its estimated value for the fictitious Aviva University. You also want to get a total for the the pledges promised. The report should look something like this:

Pledges for Aviva University

DONOR NUMBER	ITEM PROMISED	VALUE
1	Currency	100.
2	Stock	500.
.	.	.
.	.	.
		TOTAL $$$$

The command used to design reports is CREATE REPORT <name of report>. You first tell dBASE which file you are using by setting the default drive and then select the database by typing **.USE PLEDGES.** Then begin by typing **CREATE REPORT PLEDGES.** (See Figure 11.1.)

You could have called the report anything you wanted. It is okay to use the same name for the database file and the report form. In fact, it is probably preferable because it helps you remember the name (their file extensions are different: dbf for database file and frm for the report form file).

Notice the five headings on top of the screen: Options, Groups, Columns, Locate, and Exit. Options is now highlighted. Presently you see nine options. You can choose anything from the menu, as you did with the ASSIST menu. Choose any one of these options by highlighting the appropriate choice and pressing Enter. When you are done, press the Ctrl and End keys.

Now try it. Press return for Page Title. Type **Pledges for Aviva University**. Press Ctrl and then End.

NOTE: The title will be automatically centered between the left and right margins.

Choose Columns by typing **C**. Columns enables you to put in fields that you want printed on the report. The column heading contains the text that will be printed at the top of each column in the report. Press Enter on Contents. The first column will use the field DNUM. Type **DNUM** and press Enter.

(If you do not remember the spelling of the field you want, press the F10 key to get a complete list of all fields you can use and press Enter at the appropriate field.) Bring the cursor down to the heading and press Enter. The heading will be called DONORNUMBER. Type in the heading. Press Ctrl and End. The width has been filled in to 11, indicating how many spaces the report column will take when printed (to accommodate the heading). Notice on the bottom of the screen the 5 X's, representing the field width of 5 for DNUM. The >>> indicates left margins. (See Figure 11.2.)

Press PgDn to put in another field. Press Enter. Fill in for Contents: **ITEMPROMIS**. Fill in for Heading: **ITEM PROMISED**. Press PgDn to put in a third field. Fill in for Contents: **VALUE**. Fill in for Heading: **VALUE**. Press the Ctrl and End keys.

NOTE: The number of decimal places is 2; you can change it if you wish but don't. Also, the total on the bottom of the box says Yes. This can be changed to No if you wish but don't change it now.

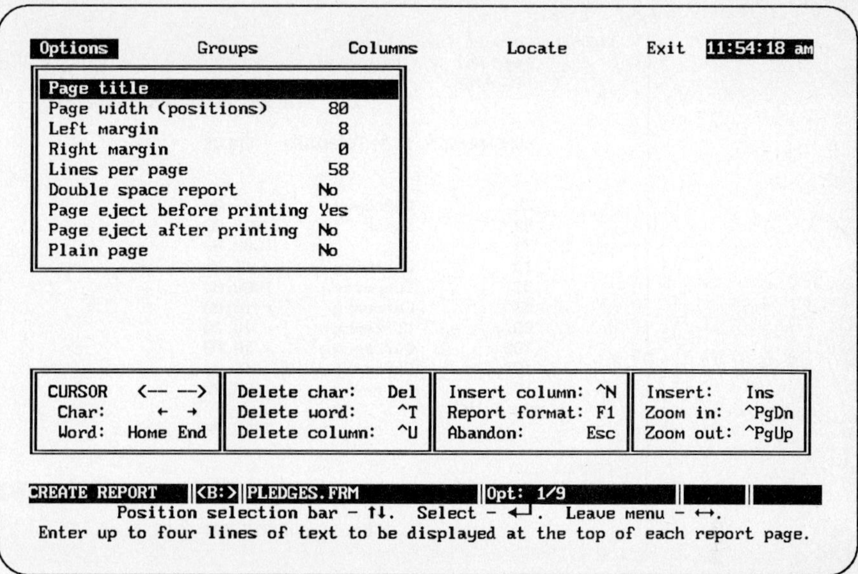

Figure 11.1 CREATE REPORT menu.

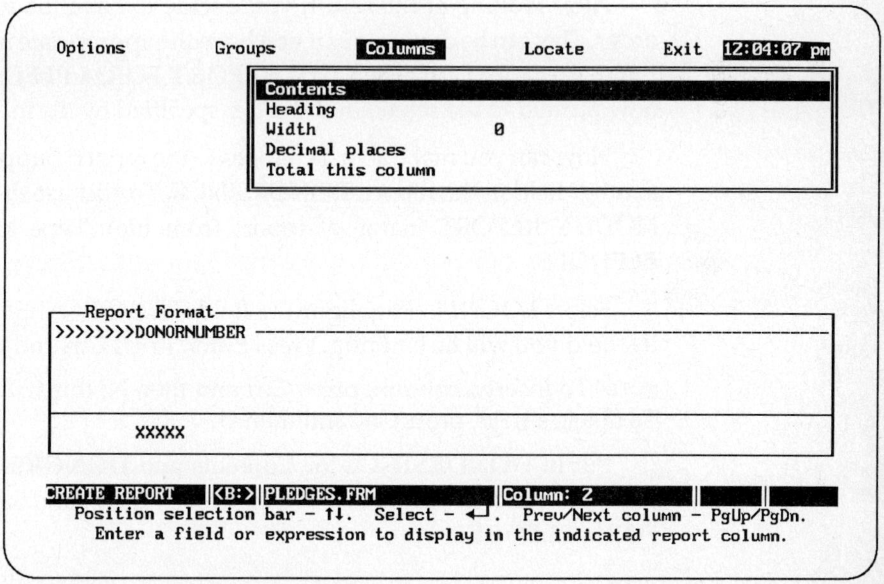

```
Options        Groups        Columns        Locate        Exit  12:04:07 pm
                           Contents
                           Heading
                           Width                   0
                           Decimal places
                           Total this column

  Report Format
>>>>>>>>DONORNUMBER --------------------------------------------------

        XXXXX

CREATE REPORT  <B:> PLEDGES.FRM          Column: 2
  Position selection bar - ↑↓.  Select - ↵.  Prev/Next column - PgUp/PgDn.
    Enter a field or expression to display in the indicated report column.
```

Figure 11.2 Report form screen with one field.

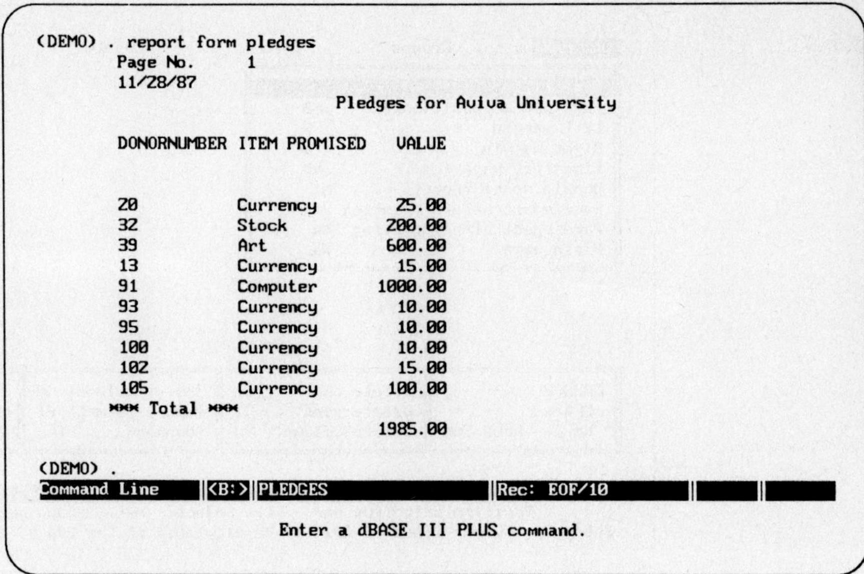

```
(DEMO) . report form pledges
       Page No.      1
       11/28/87
                             Pledges for Aviva University

       DONORNUMBER ITEM PROMISED   VALUE


       20          Currency        25.00
       32          Stock          200.00
       39          Art            600.00
       13          Currency        15.00
       91          Computer      1000.00
       93          Currency        10.00
       95          Currency        10.00
       100         Currency        10.00
       102         Currency        15.00
       105         Currency       100.00
      *** Total ***
                                 1985.00

(DEMO) .
Command Line    |<B:>|PLEDGES                |Rec: EOF/10      |    |

                       Enter a dBASE III PLUS command.
```

Figure 11.3 Report form of PLEDGES file.

Save it by choosing Exit and Save. To print the report to the screen, type **REPORT FORM PLEDGES.** (See Figure 11.3.)

After looking at the result, you decide to have the values in ascending order. This can be done easily if you have the appropriate index on. Type **.SET INDEX TO VALUE.** Then type **REPORT FORM PLEDGES.** The data are now printed to the screen in the order specified by the index.

How can you make actual changes to the report? Suppose you would like another field in the report, DONORSINCE. To edit use the command format MODIFY REPORT (name of report from file). Type **MODIFY REPORT PLEDGES.**

Select **LOCATE.** Highlight the field (ITEMPROMISE) that will precede the field you will be entering. Press Enter. Press Ctrl and then N.

NOTE: To insert a column, press Ctrl and then N; this will insert a new field. To delete a field, press Ctrl and then U.

Put in **DONORSINCE** for Contents and **DONORSINCE** for Heading. Press the Ctrl and End keys. Save by choosing Exit and Save. Type **REPORT FORM PLEDGES.**

Something Extra

If you do not want to have the date and page numbers on the report, just add the word PLAIN after the report form command (for example **REPORT FORM PLEDGES PLAIN**).

To send your report to a printer, use the command REPORT FORM **<filename of report>** TO PRINT. Type **REPORT FORM PLEDGES TO PRINT.**

NOTE: If you do not want the paper to advance a sheet when it finishes, add the word NOEJECT.

Now try a few exercises. Type. **REPORT FORM PLEDGES FOR PAIDUP.** You get a report of only the paid-up members who have pledged. Type the following:

SET INDEX TO VALUE. Enter.

REPORT FORM PLEDGES FOR DONORSINCE "1986" HEADING

"PLEDGES IN 1987 BY ALL WHO HAVE BEEN DONORS FROM BEFORE 1986". Enter.

REPORT FORM PLEDGES FOR ITEMPROMIS = "currency". Enter.

Something Extra

You can print the names and addresses in the donor file in a more compact and neater form. The first and last names can be put closer together than the way they are presently printed out by using **trim(LAST) + "," +trim(FIRST).**

First select **DONOR.** Then to build such a report, type **CREATE REPORT FORM NAMES.**

Go through the specifics. After choosing **COLUMNS**, put in

Column 1: Contents: **trim(LAST)+","+trim(FIRST);** Heading: **Donorname.**

Column 2: Contents: **Address;** Heading: **Address.**

Column 3: Contents: **CityState;** Heading: **City and State.**

Column 4: Contents: **Zip;** Heading: **ZipCode.** Exit and save.

Be sure to QUIT if you are not going on to the next lesson at this time.

12

Custom Screens

At the end of this chapter you should know how to screen and custom-design a report.

Important commands in this chapter:

- **.CREATE SCREEN <NAME>**
- **.SET FORMAT TO**

You are only just beginning to learn the power of dBASE. Before ending this beginners' introduction, let us look at a new way of appending and editing data. Until now, we were more or less confined to the way the fields were presented on the screen. Any necessary changes were based on that given format. However, dBASE lets you create the screen any way you wish in order to make it easier or more appealing to enter and manipulate data. You can custom-design the screen, which is fun.

Start dBASE and set the default drive.

Use the PLEDGES file to illustrate this. Type USE PLEDGES.

To remind yourself what the default screen looks like, type APPEND. After refreshing your memory press Esc.

```
DNUM XXXXX                PAIDUP X        DONORSINCE XXX

DATECALLED   XX/XX/XX

ITEMPROMIS   XXXXXXXXXX

PURPOSE XXXXXXXXXXXXXXX      VALUE    XXXXXXX

INFORMAT   XXXX
```

You will design a screen that looks like this.

Type **CREATE SCREEN PLEDGES.** You will be using these menus in conjunction with a "blackboard" to create the screen. To see the blackboard, press the F10 key. The blackboard is blank. To get back to the menus, press F10 again.

Go back to the blackboard. You are going to place the field names on the blackboard in any location you want. Place the field DNUM in row 2 and column 2. All you need to do is to press the down arrow two times and press the right arrow two times. You know you are at the right location since the status bar indicates row 2 col 2.

Enter **DNUM.**
Enter **PAIDUP** in row 2 column 25. Enter **DONORSINCE** in row 2 column 50.
Enter **DATECALLED** in row 5 column 2.
Enter **ITEMPROMIS** in row 8 column 2.
Enter **PURPOSE** in row 15 column 10.
Enter **VALUE** in row 15 column 50.
Enter **INFORMAT** in row 18 column 2.

To tell dBASE you are done entering the titles, press F10.

You are now back to the menus. You need to tell dBASE where the information on each field should be inserted. For example, do you want the value of DNUM to be one space or three spaces to the right of the field? You can now further custom-design the screen. To put it three spaces to the right press F10, move the cursor to row 2 column 8 and press F10 again. You are now back to the menus. Choose Modify, Content, DNUM enter, and press F10.

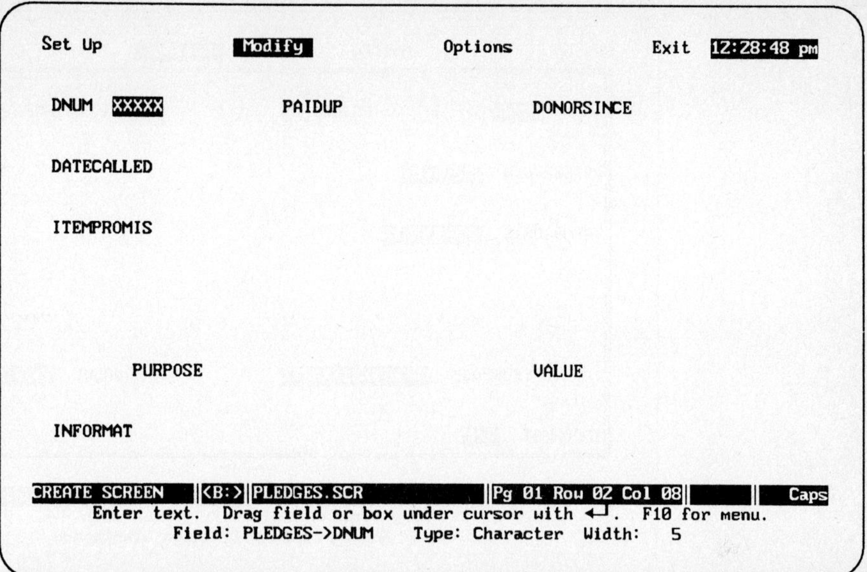

Figure 12.1

You should now see five spaces allotted for this field, indicated by the 5 X's (see Figure 12.1).

Bring the cursor to row 2 column 35 and press F10. Select Modify, Content, PAIDUP and press F10. The "L" you see represents logical, for logical operator. (When you append, either a Y, N, T, or F will be inserted.) Enter the other fields in a similar manner. Each value from the field should be three spaces to the right of the named field.

NOTE: When DATECALLED is entered, you should see 99/99/99, which represents an arbitrary date. When the VALUE contents is chosen, you should see 9999.99, showing it has five positions allotted plus two more for decimal places.

You could stop here. Instead, draw a border around all the fields. From the menu, choose Options, then Choose Double Bar. Place the cursor at row 0 column 1 and press Enter. This will anchor the cursor on the top left. Now move the cursor to row 19 column 70. This anchors the cursor on the right. Press Enter. Voilà. There's the custom screen. Press F10, choose Exit and Save (see Figure 12.2).

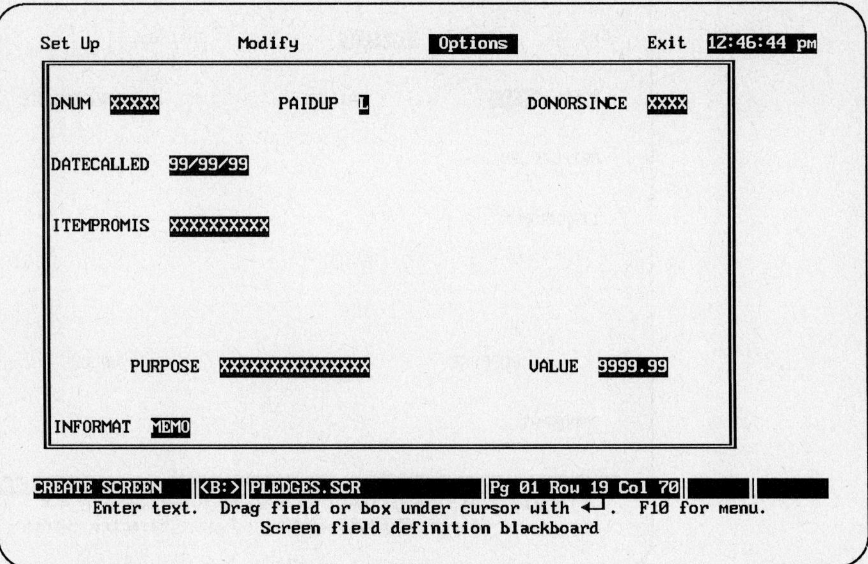

Figure 12.2

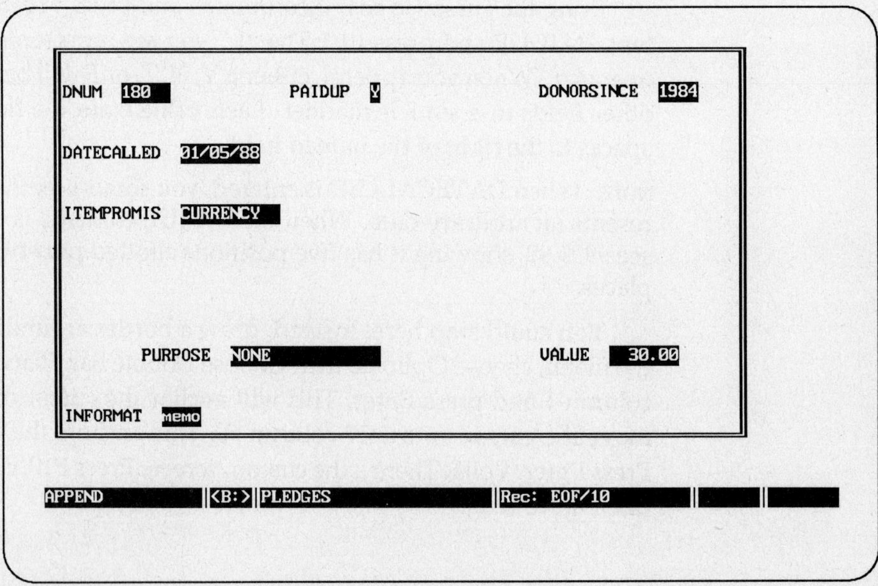

Figure 12.3

To append, type **APPEND**. Insert a new record. The DNUM is 180. He is paid-up. He has been a donor since 1984. We called him on 01/05/88, at which time he promised to give $30 for no particular purpose (see Figure 12.3).

To leave this, press Esc and type **SET FORMAT TO**. If you want to return to this custom screen at a future time, type

SET FORMAT TO <name>.

NOTE: Be careful that you enter DNUM with the proper number of leading spaces.

13

Quick Reference Guide

At the end of this chapter you should

- **know the purpose of the function keys.**
- **be familiar with 28 dBASE III PLUS commands.**

The function keys in dBASE III PLUS perform the following functions:

F1	help
F2	assist
F3	list
F4	directory
F5	display structure
F6	display status
F7	display memory
F8	display
F9	append
F10	edit

Try each of the function keys after bringing up a database such as DONOR.

28 USEFUL COMMANDS

Notation

[ ] indicates that the enclosed item is optional. Do not type in the brackets.

/ indicates a choice between options.

< > indicates that you should supply the appropriate element name within the brackets. Do not enter the brackets.

Commands in UPPERCASE should be typed exactly as shown.

Insert the appropriate element when items appear in lowercase.

1. APPEND	adds a record to the end of the file.
2. ASSIST	brings up the ASSIST menu.
3. BROWSE	displays up to seventeen records for browsing and updating.
4. CLEAR	clears the screen.
5. CREATE	sets up a new database structure.
6. CREATE REPORT	creates a report form.
7. CREATE SCREEN	creates a custom screen format using a blackboard approach.
8. DIR	shows names of dbf files.
8a. DIR *.*	shows names of all files.
9. DISPLAY ALL	shows all records from a database.
10. DISPLAY STATUS [TO PRINT]	displays current information about a database (and more) on the screen or to the printer.
11. DISPLAY STRUCTURE [TO PRINT]	displays the structure of the database file (on the screen or to the printer).
12. ERASE <filename>	removes a file from the directory.
13. GO TOP	positions the record pointer to the first record.
14. HELP	calls up the help screen.
15. LIST [TO PRINT]	lists the database records and fields.
16. MODIFY REPORT	edits a report file.

17. MODIFY STRUCTURE	alters the structure of a database.
18. PACK	permanently erases records marked for deletion.
19. QUIT	closes all dBASE files and returns you to DOS.
20. RECALL	reinstates records marked for deletion.
21. REINDEX	rebuilds existing active index files.
22. REPLACE [scope] field WITH expression [FOR condition]	changes contents of field.
23. SET DEFAULT TO	designates the default drive.
24. SET INDEX TO	opens specified index files.
25. SET PRINT ON	sends output to a printer.
26. SORT	rearranges data records in order.
27. USE	opens a database file.
28. ZAP	removes all records from a database file.

Application Exercises

Database Management Applications

Application 1

Create the following database. Sort the database in ascending order by last name. Name the file ROSTER. List its contents.

LAST	FIRST	MI	ADDRESS	CITY	STATE	ZIP
O'Kurma	Charles	D	1232 Crayton St.	Dallas	TX	75080
Dudley	Nancey	M	5342 Morgan St.	Ft. Worth	TX	76119
Raye	Susan	K	8900 Harry Hines	Dallas	TX	75223
O'Neal	Stan	J	2932 Forrest Ln.	Dallas	TX	75232
Hudspeth	Laura	P	1233 Dumont Ln.	Richardson	TX	75080
King	Carol	A	1332 Western St.	Arlington	TX	76101
Duryea	June	N	8080 Martin Dr.	Dallas	TX	75422
Spurlock	Bill	J	1919 Blair Dr.	Ft. Worth	TX	75542
Jacobs	Bryan	L	3233 Cooke Ln.	Richardson	TX	75086
Attner	Lee	V	2211 Forshee St.	Dallas	TX	75544
Patton	Terry	I	126 Dutton Dr.	Arlington	TX	76011

Application 2

Create a database giving the name, office, street address, city, state, zip code, area code, and phone number for the following people with offices in your city or state. Name the file OFFICIAL. After the database is created, locate the name of your congressman; your fire chief; your police chief.

Each senator	Your fire chief
Each congressman	Your police chief
Your mayor	Your county tax assessor
Your city manager	Your U.S. Postmaster

You may add any offices unique to your city or state or delete any not applicable.

Application 3

Create the following database. Sort the file by last name in ascending order. Name the file FACULTY. List the contents of the files.

LAST	FIRST	MI	COLLEGE	COMMITTEE	DEPARTMENT
Cox	Steven	F	Brookhaven	Auditing	Accounting
Blair	Emmeline	A	Del Mar	Registration	English
Allen	Enrique	K	Houston	Legislative	Government
Page	Michael	B	Tyler	Membership	PE
Kerr	Roger	L	Austin	Nominating	Marketing
Clere	Thomas	J	Houston	Registration	English
Green	Lawanda	W	Weatherford	Membership	Drama
Hurst	Edith	I	Midland	Resolutions	Accounting
Cox	Leticia	R	El Centro	Auditing	Art
Hall	Alden	P	Hill County	Social	Mathematics
Ford	Alyce	A	Brazosport	Editorial	Reading
Lobb	Gerald	C	Odessa	Editorial	Physics

Peters	Leroy	B	Houston	Social	History
Bailey	Joyce	R	San Antonio	Legislative	English
Burns	Linda	M	St Phillips	Auditing	PE

Application 4

Add the following employees to the file named ROSTER; then resort the file in ascending order by last name.

LAST	FIRST	MI	ADDRESS	CITY	STATE	ZIP
Brown	Janet	K	2211 Hilcrest St.	Ft. Worth	TX	76244
Grant	Hazel	T	201 Jackson St.	Ft. Worth	TX	76787
Puerta	Maria	I	477 Campus Dr.	Ft. Worth	TX	76119
Jones	Peggy	S	909 Beckley Dr.	Ft. Worth	TX	76331
Jacobs	Billy	V	551 Riverside Dr.	Ft. Worth	TX	76001

Application 5

Retrieve the file named FACULTY and delete all members of the Editorial Committee. Save the file again under the same name.

Application 6

Create the following database using columns A to C. Sort the database in ascending order by city office. Name the file PUBLIC. Generate a report which will show the following.

DUNCANVILLE, TEXAS

City Hall

Duncanville, TX 75033

CITY OFFICE	PHONE NO.	NAME
City Manager	780-5017	Kevin Smith
Assistant City Manager	780-4000	Betty Cimeron

City Secretary	780-5004	Jim Davis
Director of Finance	780-5005	Ruth Willis
Director of Personnel	780-5070	Janet Morgan
Director of Purchasing	780-0001	Brent Woodward
Tax Office	780-3211	Dianna Harwood
Fire chief	780-2333	John Willingham
Police Chief	780-2020	Ralph Harris
Director of Public Works	780-3233	Jess Parkhill

Application 7

Create the following database. Name the file TITLES.

MORGAN PUBLISHING COMPANY

Title Index

TITLE	AUTHOR	COPYRIGHT
Affluent Americans	Winters, R. R.	1985
Auditing Made Easy	Jeters, P. L.	1985
Business: Tomorrow's Future	Ramsey, J. T.	1988
Contemporary Business Relations	Zimmerman, L.I.	1988
Essentials of Business	Hartley, F. M.	1989
Fundamentals of Management	Cullen, R. W.	1988
Practical Administration	Venzor, R. Q.	1989

Insert a record after "Contemporary Business Relations" and add the following information under each appropriate heading:

TITLE	AUTHOR	COPYRIGHT
Delusion: The American Economy	Winters, R. R.	1989

Application 8

Retrieve the file named TITLES. Sort the author's names in ascending order. Add a field after "AUTHOR", title it COPIESSOLD. Leave it blank.

Application 9

Create the following database. Sort the database in ascending order. Name the file WILSON. Extract the names of those people who watched "One is Enough" on July 15. Generate a report of this information.

WILSON TV RATINGS

775 Corrigan Avenue, San Jose, Ca 95334

July 15, 19--

NAME	TIME	TV SHOW WATCHED	NETWORK
Wilson, George	7:00	One is Enough	CBC
Wilson, George	7:30	Run for Your Money	NBB
Sanders, Maria	6:00	Bad Day in Georgetown	NBB
Sanders, Maria	7:30	Great is My Worth	NBB
McAvoy, Bill	8:00	Best of Everything	CBC
McAvoy, Bill	8:30	You Are For Me	CBC
Martin, J. T.	6:30	Bet Your Savings	NBB
Kennedy, B.T.	7:00	One is Enough	CBC
Kennedy, B.T.	7:30	Run for Your Money	NBB
Rutledge, R. R.	7:00	One is Enough	CBC
Rutledge, R. R.	7:30	Wheel of Tomorrow	AAB
Lewis, Mark	7:00	One is Enough	CBC
Bryan, F. D.	8:00	The Betty Sutton Story	NBB

Application 10

Create the following database. Name the file RENTERS. Extract and print one copy of the names of the renters who pay only on the first of the month; the first and fifteenth; and the fifteenth of the month.

HILLTOP APARTMENTS
4233 Hilltop Drive
Union, NJ 07083

NAME	APT	BLDG.	TYPE	RENT	DUE
James, W. Bill	101	A	2 bdrm, 2 bath	$440	1
Lee, James J.	102	A	2 bdrm, 1 bath	$350	1
Harris, Jeffry	103	A	2 bdrm, 1 bath	$350	1 & 15
Key, John	104	A	2 bdrm, 2 bath	$440	15
Sammons, Betty	201	B	1 bdrm, 1 bath	$300	1 & 15
Judson, A. L.	202	B	1 bdrm, 1 bath	$300	15
Daniels, Joe	203	B	1 bdrm, 1 bath	$300	1 & 15
Wheat, William	204	B	1 bdrm, 1 bath	$300	1 & 15

Application 11

Create the following database. Index the file by name in ascending order and print one copy. Name the file RETIRE. Sort the file by date retired and print one copy.

BELL MANUFACTURING COMPANY
DIVISION OF DATATRON
1190 Regents Parkway
Burleson, TX 76028-2399
Retirement Report, December 31, 19--

NAME	DEPARTMENT	YEAR RETIRED
Sartain, J. J.	Personnel	1980
Cockerham, Dianne	Engineering	1979
Johnston, Jr., N. E.	Marketing	1951
Reed, Joey	Maintenance	1965
Allen, William	Communications	1977
Hairston, Carlos	Safety	1984
Gladden, W. W.	Purchasing	1966
Murphy, Carol A.	Engineering	1988
Shockley, Durward	Marketing	1990

Application 12

Create the following database. Name the file SEMINAR. Generate a report that prints each speaker a copy of his/her schedule.

HOUSMAN FINANCIAL PLANNERS

Family Financial Program Seminar

July 22, 19--

TOPIC	SPEAKER	NUMBER	TIME	ROOM
Family Financial Programs	Williams	22	9:00	101
Common Stocks	Bailey	18	9:00	206
Investment Funds	Davis	24	9:00	211
Real Estate	Williams	15	10:00	121
Savings Accounts	Bailey	12	10:00	206
Inflation	Davis	18	10:00	106
Life Insurance	Williams	18	1:00	101
Individual Retirement Accounts	Bailey	23	1:00	206
Other Tax Shelters	Davis	20	1:00	106
Military Retirement/Separation	Williams	10	2:00	106
Other Subjects of Interest	Bailey	12	2:00	101

Application 13

Create the following database. Index the file by last name in ascending order. Name the file MORGAN. Search and find the customers with a $2,000 credit limit. Generate a report that will produce the following output.

MORGAN BRYANT

2144 Johnson Parkway

Arlington, Tx 76013-6246

Customer List, Arlington

NAME	ADDRESS	ACCT NO	CR LIMIT
Brock, Bill	221 Crestmont St.	6060-10	$ 1000
Vaughan, Frank	114 Ridgeway St.	6022-34	$ 500
Fulton, Mildred	875 Morgan Dr.	6033-63	$ 1500
Miller, Ruth P.	909 Reading Ln.	6026-89	$ 1000
Parks, Donald	1212 Brandon Dr.	6033-33	$ 300
Thomas, Malcolm	1514 Beardon St.	6077-21	$ 2000
Trout, Ira	322 Pendelton St.	6021-16	$ 500
Laird, Bertha	199 Hargrove Dr.	6038-09	$ 2000
Boothe, Margaret	221 Bennington Ln.	6022-88	$ 1500
Finch, Ethel	9986 Portland St.	6066-29	$ 300

Application 14

Retrieve the file named MORGAN. Insert a column after "ACCT NO" and insert the following information:

ACCT BALANCE

$ 449.60

$ 322.00

$1090.55

$ 950.25

$ 185.13

$1933.56

$ 449.66

$ 87.05

$ 326.80

$ 72.11

Save the file again under the name MORGAN. Generate a new report.

Index